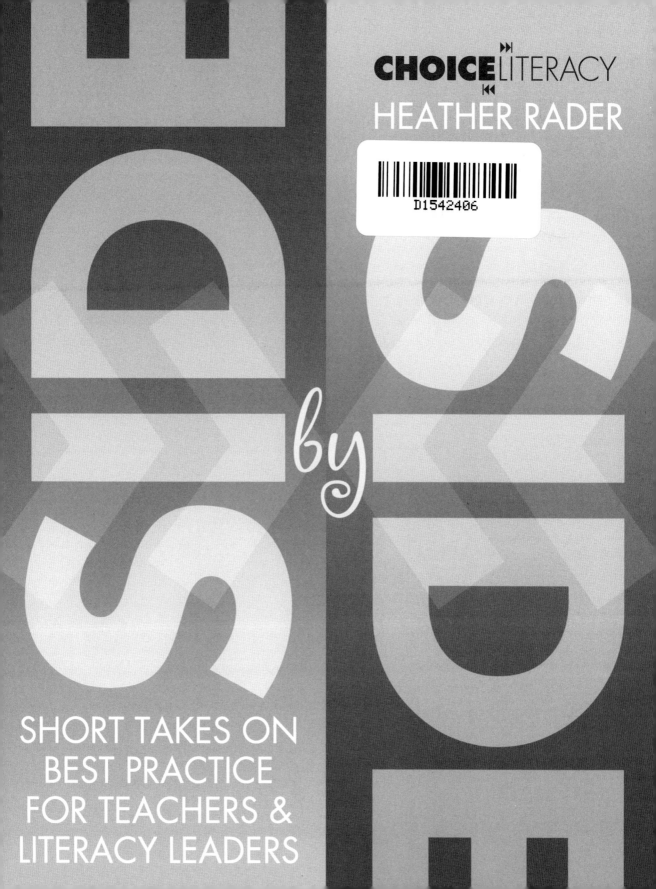

SIDE by SIDE

CHOICE LITERACY
HEATHER RADER

SHORT TAKES ON
BEST PRACTICE
FOR TEACHERS &
LITERACY LEADERS

Choice Literacy, P.O. Box 790, Holden, Maine 04429
www.choiceliteracy.com

Library of Congress Cataloging in Publication Data Pending

ISBN 978-1-60155-036-1

Cover and interior design by Martha Drury
Manufactured in the United States of America

17 16 15 14 13 12   9 8 7 6 5 4 3 2 1

To Ahna, Jamin, and Maya

You are.
And always will be.
My best teachers.

Contents

Part 3: Explicitly Teaching Writing   102

Part 4: Assessing What Matters   144

Foreword

by Brenda Power

Peek into one of the many classrooms where Heather Rader spends her days and you might have trouble figuring out what her job is. At any given moment, you could see her kneeling beside a student, listening carefully to the child read his writing draft. Classroom aide? Yet in the next hour, in another classroom, Heather might be at the front of the room, teaching a lesson on nonfiction text features. Must be the teacher, right? Yet an hour or two later, there she is at a conference table with a gaggle of teachers, leading a discussion as everyone pores over reams of assessment data and student work samples. Principal? Curriculum coordinator?

Heather Rader is an instructional coach, and a remarkable one at that. Many literacy coaches talk about how the job can feel like a "no-man's-land." No longer teachers, and not administrators, they are challenged to create an identity with meaning and purpose, often without much direction from others. Heather has found her identity by staying true to a few core principles, which are infused throughout her writing. Heather believes these things:

Every teacher deserves a coach.
You can't coach someone who doesn't want to be coached.
Coaches take many different stances (collaborating, consulting, coaching), and fit matters.
Listening is the most important tool, and talking is highly overrated.

But when talking, impeccability matters.
Approximation rules.
Taking care of yourself allows you to care for others.

With warmth, humor, and a steely will, Heather shows these beliefs in action throughout the essays in *Side by Side*. I've had the pleasure of seeing these stories of teaching and learning emerge over the past two years as Heather has shared them with Choice Literacy readers at www.choiceliteracy.com. Literacy coaches and teachers see themselves in Heather's experiences, because there is such honesty throughout about the awkwardness of being a guest in someone's classroom, negotiating a role, and getting to know each other amidst twenty-five to thirty students who have needs, right here and right now.

This book is designed to move literacy coaching from a no-man's-land to everyone's territory. The message from Heather throughout is that we are all in this together. Let's be kind, and with a little humility and humor, we can find joy in working together every day.

Each topic includes a pair of essays—one from the classroom teacher's perspective and the other with guidance for literacy coaches. Because Heather's work is so rooted in classrooms, the mix is eclectic (just like the issues that come up every day in schools). Tackling everything from sarcasm to writing prompts, Heather moves gracefully between teachers and coaches, children and lessons, nudging readers to think and think again about their role in collaborating with colleagues. The essays are brief, and could easily be read aloud in staff or grade-level team meetings as ice-breakers or to spark conversations. The number of paired essays is also ideal for reading one topic a week throughout the school year in study groups. Reflection questions at the end of each essay might leave you itching to write in your teaching journal, or provoke some spirited talk with colleagues.

One of my pet peeves is the abundance of negativity in our profession. And it's true—there is plenty to whine about in education. From poor wages to impossible conditions, there is lots of evidence to support anyone who says the job can't be done well. The reason we see brilliant teaching and learning going on every day anyway, in every school, is because of people like Heather who refuse to accept negativity. In the last essay in the book, Heather writes the following:

> *I take a challenging interaction, a critical e-mail or even someone rolling their eyes in a meeting, and I turn it around and send it off in a positive way. "When you are grateful, fear disappears and abundance appears" is a quote from Anthony Robbins that describes my experience. Every person in general and teachers in particular benefit from an attitude of gratitude.*

I am grateful for educators like Heather, who not only teaches beautifully, but writes about her experiences with such a lovely, light touch. I am also grateful to you. I suspect since you're holding this book in your hands now, you're one of those brilliant folks who time and again finds ways to send teachers and kids off in positive ways, no matter what the world throws at you. I'm delighted you've found your way to Heather's words. Prepare to meet a kindred spirit in these pages.

Acknowledgments

A number of these short takes were first published electronically with Choice Literacy, but they would never have found their way into the pages of a book without the belief and investment of Brenda Power. From our shared feelings about dogs to our love of words, how wonderful it is to work side by side with "power."

Another person who believed in me as a teacher-writer long before I did is Joe Belmonte. Thank you, and I think it's my turn to treat for sushi.

To my Compass Girls, Beth and Lu, your listening and care are embedded in every page of this book.

Special thanks to the best coaching team (past and present) in the world at North Thurston: Amanda "Mandi" Adrian, Becky Lee, Colleen Miller, Cristina Charney, Dixie Reimer, Donnita Hawkins, Emily Aufort, Janeal Maxfield, Jami Roberts, Jenna Tate, Kevin Gary, Kris Andrews-Brown, Linda Karamatic, Megan Conklin, Meghan Ohumikini, Vikki Voss, Scott Haury, and of course the other Heather, Heather Sisson.

Thank you to the wonderful colleagues at North Thurston who have opened up their classrooms and taught me how to be a coach. My dad was the first, many years ago. Cheers to the fine educators in the Teachers as Writers group—you remind me why writing together is so much better. And another toast to the Center for Strengthening the Teaching Profession (CSTP) that gave me time, space, and great food to write my first "short takes."

Thank you to the Choice Literacy contributors who inspire me, and to Katherine Casey Spengler for connecting me in the first place.

Thank you to Laurel Robinson for crossing my t's, dotting my i's, and patiently redirecting my verb tenses. Thank you to Martha Drury for taking my text and telling the visual story. Thank you to Shelly Hafford for taking care of all the details and having a great sense of humor.

To my Mom (also known as Nana), Brunca, and Pop, thank you for being there for our deluxe editions while I worked on this book—and taxiing them everywhere. You made this possible.

And finally to my husband, Kurt, who dared me to try to publish an article in 1998. I'm thankful I lost that bet and for your gift of Saturdays. I went on to set a wildly improbable goal that I'd publish a book before I turned forty—I turn forty next month.

Starting Out Effective

Sarcasm Sets a Great Tone—NOT

Teacher: [*to her sixth graders*] Take out your pencils and your journals.
Student: I can't find my journal.
Teacher: What a surprise, because you are always such a neatnik. Do you think people are going to follow you around cleaning up after you for the rest of your life?
[*Other students in the group laugh and look at the overflowing desk and one repeats, "Neatnik."*]

In general during my early years as an instructional coach, I was surprised at the pervasive use of sarcasm in the elementary classroom, but in particular I noticed a high correlation between sarcastic teachers and their classroom-management difficulties. The consequences for using sarcasm with students are many.

Sarcasm is a virus. It starts with the teacher and quickly spreads student-to-student. Bernice was the teacher speaking in the opening excerpt, and she told me her classroom culture was poisonous; the kids were cruel to her and to each other. Sure enough, within five minutes of being in her room transcribing on my laptop, a kid leaned back in his chair and said to me in a hardened tone, "This class totally sucks." Bernice was right on about the toxicity; however, she didn't see her role in its development.

Bernice's classroom rules say, "We do not use put-downs in this classroom," but her behavior contradicted the norm. The student was obviously not neat, so the teacher was saying, "You are a slob" under the guise of sarcasm. In this case sarcasm was the surrogate for underlying, less acceptable emotions such as frustration, anger, disappointment, or confusion. From the look on the student's face, my interpretation was that he heard it as a put-down and proceeded to disrupt the lesson by poking his neighbor with a pencil. The same student later made a sarcastic comment when a group member shared her personal writing out loud.

Technically, *sarcasm* is defined in the *American Heritage Dictionary* as "a cutting, often ironic remark intended to wound" and "a form of wit that is marked by the use of sarcastic language and is intended to make its victim the butt of contempt or ridicule." From its Latin and Greek roots it means "to bite the lips in rage."

4

These words—*wound, victim,* and *rage*—suggest that the speaker has poor intentions. On the contrary, I don't believe any teacher gets up in the morning and says, "I'm going to go be a negative influence in the lives of children today." Not at all. So why do teachers use sarcasm with kids? In our conversations here is what they tell me:

"I grew up with it. I don't even really notice it."

"The kids hear it on the sitcoms, and they use it with each other. They get it."

"The kids think it's funny."

Sarcasm is typically funniest to the speaker. Comedian Lucas Molandes in his show *Live at Gotham* poses this question to the audience: "Do you remember in your relationship when sarcasm was funny? And then at one point it turns into mean, insightful commentary on the other person's failures as a human being." When we use sarcasm as a veil for venting and name calling, we communicate our negative observations without risk because we can always follow up with, "It was just a joke."

Golden Rule

It's so basic: do unto others as you would have done unto you, the ultimate ethic of reciprocity. My friend and colleague Katie Baydo-Reed wrote about her toughest year of teaching in an essay for Choice Literacy called "On Compassion" (2011). "After several months, it began to wear on me. I must admit their behavior did not spawn in a total vacuum. It was inexcusable, but I engaged in belittling, sarcastic behavior as I attempted to shame students into compliance. Together, my students and I had established a classroom utterly devoid of respect—a toxic environment if there ever was one." What did she do to make a change? She acknowledged her behavior, wrote each student a letter, looked for something positive in each day, and refused to resort to sarcasm and humiliation. She's still teaching and works to live up to her own expectations each day, not perfectly, but willingly. In other words, she started treating students the way she wanted them to treat her.

It's one thing to establish what we believe is unbecoming to our profession when we aren't actually teaching. Before student teaching and my subsequent teaching jobs, I was never going to lose my temper. Ha! Just like before becoming a parent I wasn't ever going to sit my kid in front of the television as a babysitter. Ha ha! But once we are actually teaching, it's important to establish our expectations, not just of the students, but of ourselves.

Ask Yourself

Do you want students to call you names and humiliate each other? In turn, will you use sarcasm with them instead of speaking honestly?

Do you want students to address you with concerns in front of the whole class or privately? In turn, will you address them privately with concerns?

Do you want students to yell at you and each other? In turn, will you yell at them?

Do you want kids to think that writing is a punishment? In turn, will you punish them with writing?

Do you want students to take away your ability to get exercise and fresh air? In turn, will you take away their recesses?

Do you want your whole staff punished if only one or two teachers are misbehaving? In turn, will you punish your whole class instead of pinpointing the behavior of individuals?

Getting clear on what tone you want set in your classroom and your ultimate role in setting that tone can help define your philosophy that you share with students and parents. "I don't believe in bad kids" was one I shared publicly. I didn't use that language to describe kids who struggled with behaviors, nor did I allow students to use it about each other or other educators to use it about my students. I also was not a yeller. I vowed to raise my voice only when there was a safety concern and I needed to get kids' attention quickly. These were things I told my students the first days of school: "In this classroom you can expect me not to yell, and in turn I'll expect you . . ."

Communicating with Families

We can take a strengths-based or deficit-based look at students from the very start. The first few days and weeks of school, I voraciously wrote notes about what I noticed students doing well in the classroom. By the third week of school I had called every family and shared something I genuinely appreciated about their child. After their initial concern about why I was calling, I'd hear from parents, "This is the first positive call I've ever received about my son or daughter. Thank you."

Yes, it's an investment of time, especially those first busy weeks of school. And yes, it makes a big difference in setting the tone. When I had to call families at other points in the year to discuss behavior concerns, we already had a positive foundation set.

How will you set the tone this school year? This week? This moment? When will you begin? If you haven't set a tone you are proud of, may you have the strength to start again.

A Coach's Perspective: Is Sarcasm in Style This Season?

"What surprises you when you hear me read your lesson aloud?" I asked Courtney in our debrief.

"Well, I guess it sounds like I'm rude to the students . . . at least on paper," she responded.

"On paper?" I asked.

"Yes, where I'm being sarcastic with the kids. Sarcasm is just the way I am, though; it's part of my teaching style."

Sarcasm isn't a teaching style, I fought the urge to say. Right then and there, I wanted to tell her how when we talk down to our students, we are modeling poor communication that we'll later attempt to abolish when they use it with each other in class. I wanted to cite Marzano, Pickering and Marzano's research from *Classroom Management That Works: Research-Based Strategies for Every Teacher* (2003) to prove that kids don't respond well to sarcasm. Mostly I wanted to tell her how painful it was for me to sit in her room for forty minutes like an accomplice, recording it all on a transcript.

But that is only the bubble above my head. Instead, I listen with curiosity. I want to understand how Courtney as a fresh, exuberant first-year teacher has come to this decision that sarcasm is an acceptable "teaching style." I write in my notes "rude on paper" and "sarcasm/style" to remember her words precisely. I am her coach. The only way we are going to be able to work together and establish a working relationship is if I trust her and she trusts me. Judgment degrades trust. So I put it aside—for now.

This isn't the first time I've encountered sarcasm in the classroom, and although these are fifth graders, I've heard it all the way down to classrooms of five-year-olds. Like a Magic Eye picture that begins to emerge as I relax my focus, I see a positive correlation between teachers' resistance to coaching and their struggles with classroom management. A commonality I've found among teachers struggling with classroom management is the element of sarcasm in their classrooms.

As a coach, sometimes the end of the school day represents the beginning of my workday. I look at transcripts from Courtney's room, and honestly I am thinking, *What the heck do I do next?* For moments like these, I've tucked little inspirational quotes around my office:

> *I've come to the frightening conclusion that I am the decisive element in the classroom. It's my personal approach that creates the climate. It's my daily mood that makes the weather. As a teacher, I possess tremendous power to make a student's life miserable or joyous. I can be a tool of torture or an instrument of inspiration. I can humiliate or humor, hurt or heal. In all situations it is my response that decides whether a crisis will be escalated or de-escalated and a student humanized or de-humanized. (Ginott, Ginott, and Goddard 2003, 76)*

I begin my reflection by asking myself, *What can I do to give Courtney another perspective on how she, as the decisive element in her room, is daily creating the climate that ultimately only she can affect?* Changing the level of sarcasm in her classroom is no small task. It will change only if she wants it to.

One of the myths I operated under during my first year of coaching was that teachers knew how and what to observe. I thought, *They can surely see what I see.* I was wrong. I replaced that belief with, *If I tell them what I see, they will be able to see it.* Wrong again. Currently, I share with new coaches, "It doesn't matter what you see if they don't see it," so the first step is to create a common context.

Common Context Using Transcripts

There are many ways to have a conversation about an interaction or lesson. My personal preference in a situation like this that involves inspecting language is to use transcripts. I transcribe lessons on my laptop and have the script available on the screen or printed off to use to debrief with the teacher. I use a "nothing but the facts, ma'am, approach" to my transcripts. Students will often wander behind me and are surprised to see me getting down what is being said in the moment. I explain to teachers that it is simply like taking a snapshot, so we have something to look at together to discuss and so I don't have to remember it all.

When I debrief, I prefer to give the teacher a copy and read it out loud at the same time. Before I begin reading, I revisit the purpose that the teacher and I collaboratively set for that observation. If the teacher has asked me to look at classroom management, I might simply say, "When I read this aloud, think about our focus on classroom management," and then I matter-of-factly read the transcript.

Dynamic Dialogue

A little mantra I repeat as a coach is "listen, talk, listen," which reminds me that I should be listening about two-thirds of the time. Still, I prepare my first questions to propel our conversation. Let's return now to Courtney's transcript. Courtney was a first-year, fifth-grade teacher, and we had been in a coaching cycle for a few weeks. She expressed being excited to have me in her room, and I felt like there was the beginning of trust between us. This is an excerpt from the transcript I read to her:

Teacher. OK, take out your passages and read along while I read it to you. Remember we are working on providing text-based evidence for our inferences. Eric Santos, why are you talking?

Student. I'm asking Teresa if she can get Quinton's book because he's gone.

Teacher. Where is yours?

Student. I left it at home.

Teacher. You are quite the mooch, aren't you? Put your name up.

Student. Why?

Teacher. Not being prepared to learn. Rule number one, Mr. Santos.
[*Student noise level begins to rise.*]

Teacher. You guys are like a bunch of little first graders. The minute I turn my attention, you get out of control. Seriously, sometimes I feel like I'm student teaching again.
[*Teacher reads passage.*]

Teacher. So what are you inferring that the character is feeling about now? Chelsea?

Student. The daughter?

Teacher. No, the guy next door. Yes, of course the daughter.

After I finished reading the transcript with Courtney, I asked her, "What surprises you when you hear me read your lesson aloud?" She told me a lot about herself as a teacher when she said, "Sarcasm is my teaching style." I now knew that she was aware of it, but that it appeared rude only on paper. In reality, she believed, her fifth graders liked relating on an adult level. We went on to discuss other aspects of making inferences and stayed focused on the students.

The next week I came back and said, "You know, I've been doing some thinking about how you said that the sarcasm sounded rude on paper. I wonder if some of the frustration you are having with the way your students are talking to each other could be connected to that."

Courtney sighed. "It could be. I could probably get better at that. I've started noticing it more now too when I looked back at that transcript."

"What would you want it to sound like?"

"I just don't want to be so negative with them. Especially in the morning, because it just goes downhill in the afternoon. I noticed in that prediction lesson how you ignored a few of their comments and the comments stopped. And you were so positive with them even when they didn't get it."

In the last minutes of our meeting, I summarized our conversation and tried to get a sense of what Courtney was taking away:

"I heard that you were considering trying to ignore more of the student behaviors to see if it causes them to decrease. I was also thinking that redirecting seems to work well like when you said, 'I'll answer your question when you raise your hand.' That was definitely keeping it positive while still having high expectations. If you'd like, I can watch for more examples when I'm here on Friday. What was something you took away from our meeting today?"

Courtney said, "I thought you and I were only going to be talking about reading, but we've talked a lot about management stuff because it is getting in the way."

Noticing and Validating

The next week, I noticed several times that Courtney was ignoring some student behaviors and positively redirecting kids instead of responding with sarcasm.

Student: What page are we on?
Teacher: Use your resources; quietly check with a neighbor.

As the students filed out for music, I said, "You disengaged from the page-number power struggle and kept everyone on track."

She grinned and said, "I could totally hear your voice in the back of my head saying, 'Redirect, redirect, redirect.' And it worked."

Truth Telling

Several weeks into our coaching cycle came the moment when Courtney asked me, "Do you think I use too much sarcasm with my students?"

I wanted to ask, "Do you think you do? Because that's what matters." But I could see something in her expression that was trusting and vulnerable and wanted . . . the truth. She knew the truth, but she wanted my validation.

"I think," I began carefully, "that when you use sarcasm, you don't get the results from kids that you want."

She was quiet for a minute and said, "Yeah, I think that too."

Sar-Caustic

Courtney's principal called me a few weeks after our coaching cycle ended. My work with teachers is completely confidential, so the only thing I report to principals is my schedule (for accountability) and the content area we are focused on. Any reports of "How is it going?" come from what the teacher chooses to share, not me.

"I just wanted to tell you that Courtney is greeting kids outside her classroom now and saying something positive to each one before they walk through the door," the principal said. "Her whole attitude toward kids and teaching seems to have shifted significantly. She's a lot less caustic. I don't know what you did, but it is working for her."

After I got off the phone, I considered the word he had used—*caustic*—and thought how it is defined as destroying something living. As a coach I have been surprised by the pervasive use of sarcasm in classrooms of teachers who struggle to manage their classes. I don't know exactly what worked for Courtney in our coaching connection, but I would bet it had to do with suspending judgment and patiently waiting for her to consider another perspective from a trusted colleague. I'm constantly humbled and honored by this work; teachers have an amazing capacity to both resist and embrace change. Sarcasm is no longer in style in Courtney's class.

Consider These Questions

What connections do you make when you read the inspirational quote?

How do you create a common context with teachers?

How might the outcome of the coaching cycle have been different if the coach had told Courtney she was being sarcastic from the beginning?

What is a situation in which you've been asked by a teacher for the truth? How much did you share? How did you say it?

Who Rules? Creating a Classroom Code of Conduct

Once a year, I created a teacher report card for my students. Some of the most interesting feedback I got came from two continua that I asked students to place me on.

Easy_____Strict
Unjust _____Fair

The majority of my students, no matter which grade level I taught, rated me on the right pole of the axes: highly strict and highly fair. Students wrote things like, "She doesn't let us get away with not learning" and "Everybody gets to make the rules, but she makes sure everybody follows them."

I was surprised that my classes thought of me as strict, but I realized it was their way of saying that behavior expectations were clear, predictable, and consistent in our room. Over the years I developed a system for getting students' input on a social contract, which was an important starting component for our work together.

Brainstorming the Rules

I began by holding up a well-known childhood game board like Candyland. After modeling what it meant to turn to a partner and take turns sharing ideas, I gave the students a minute to recall all the rules from Candyland they could remember.

"You turn the cards upside down on the board."

"If you get the molasses one, you have to go back."

"Two colors means you get to go two of those color squares."

"If you find the Candy Castle first, you win."

I said to the class, "I wonder what would happen if there were no rules for Candyland."

One student said, "People might just pick the cards they want."

Another added, "People would cheat."

"It wouldn't be any fun," mused a third, "because the winner wouldn't really be the winner."

"In our classroom," I said, "we are going to have clear rules like Candyland so everyone knows how to play and everyone can feel like a winner."

I then had them turn back to their partner and brainstorm rules they thought we might need in our classroom. After that they had quiet independent time to write down rules and then pick the most important one.

Choosing the Rules

Before the next session, I wrote each student's most important rule on chart paper. There were seven "Keep hands and feet to yourself" and five "Treat others the way you want to be treated," so I wrote those only once. In total there were thirteen different rules.

As I pulled out the rules for Candyland, I showed them the five game rules and said, "I wonder what would happen if there were fifty rules for Candyland."

Hands shot up. "No one would remember them."

A little boy with glasses pushed them up on his nose and added, "I can say for absolutely sure that I wouldn't play because that sounds like Chest and there is too many rules."

"Yes," I said, chuckling. "Chessss . . . can be a challenge."

Pointing to the chart paper I said, "Even thirteen rules seems like a lot to remember, so I'd like us to vote to choose our top five-to-seven rules."

I handed each student three colorful sticky dots and told them they could spend them in three ways: all the dots on one rule, two dots on one rule and one dot on another, or one dot on each of three rules.

A couple of students modeled selecting rules, and we talked about choosing what we thought was best for the class (as well as the importance of not covering up anyone else's dots).

At the end of our vote, we had six clear winners, and these became our classroom rules. At that point I acted as the scribe for shared writing as we checked to be sure all our choices were written positively instead of negatively. For example, we rewrote, "Don't do sloppy work" as "Try your best." Every rule started off with "In Mrs. R's class, we choose to . . ."

Acknowledgments and Consequences

"Most of the time in Candyland you get to move forward, but sometimes you have to go back. Just like with our classroom choices, most of the time most of you will follow most of the rules. But if you don't, I want you to know what you are choosing instead. You are going to help come up with fair consequences for the classroom, but I need you to know I don't embarrass kids, hurt kids, or punish with writing."

Students paired up and brainstormed consequences. I was always surprised by how hard they were as disciplinarians. It was not unusual to hear someone suggest, "Lose all recesses for a whole week." Ouch! That punishes everyone.

I wrote down their suggestions and told them I would consider them all and then choose a few that ranged from light consequences to more serious consequences. Almost every year they were similar: *reminder, time-out, call home, remove from room, go to office.* Yet it was important that we were all part of the process.

"It's also important to acknowledge the people who are following the rules," I said. "When I notice classmates following rules, I will give them a ticket, and after they write their name on it, they can put the ticket in this jar. Every Friday I'll pull some tickets so we can acknowledge a few of our classmates for making choices that help us all learn."

"I don't acknowledge kids with food, gifts, or letting them skip homework," I said. Again, within those parameters they brainstormed acknowledgments, from getting to sit in my rolling chair for a day, to sitting by a friend at lunch, to—I kid you not—getting to be the whiteboard eraser for a week. Although I may not have predicted all these motivators, kids were getting excited about the creative possibilities. Of those I chose a short menu of five.

Ratifying and Living the Contract

"The people at Milton Bradley [now Hasbro] had to all agree on the rules for Candyland," I said. "We are going to read over our choices, consequences, and acknowledgments, and then I have a fine-tipped Sharpie at each table for us all to sign if you agree. Your parents are going to sign a copy of this too when it goes home with the newsletter."

We clapped when it was all signed, and then picked places around the room to post our enlarged 11-by-17-inch rule sheets.

We continually revisited the classroom choices. At multiple points throughout the year we had to refocus. For example, "In this class we choose to listen to each other's ideas." I'd make a chart. "What does that look like? What does that sound like? How are we doing on a four-three-two-one scale? How can we improve?"

Although some days I believe I was a warmhearted Queen Frostine and other days maybe more like Gramma Nutt or even Lord Licorice, starting out with a clear agreement helped us experience the Candyland motto: "The best part of playing is playing together."

Consider These Questions

Have you considered having your students fill out a report card for you? What would you want to know?

What is the value of involving students in the process of writing rules versus having them up and ready to go on the first day of class?

What are the steps of your social contracts process? Is there something you'd like to add or change?

Coaching Out of Chaos

One of my friends is a highly creative type with many big ideas. The other night he was talking about website design, and wondering aloud if he created a business card that read, "I'll START your website," consumers would bite. Another imaginarian spoke up: "And I could be the closer. I'm great at coming in for short periods of time and rescuing things that get messed up."

"Who," I asked, "will do the work of maintaining?"

They were thoughtful for a moment and then one said, "That's really overrated." We laughed.

It's true that coming up with an idea is engaging, and many of us are full of energy when we plan new projects. It's a time for dreaming and scheming. However, the day-to-day work of maintaining a system requires heads-down dedication and fortitude. In other words, consistency is the key to any working system.

Working Together

Mara Mason (a pseudonym) was a first-year teacher who had been assigned a wonderful mentor, Nancy, the teacher next door. In the beginning, all was well with Mara. She had a pretty bulletin board for her self-created rules, and she rarely had to refer to it. I heard from Nancy first in October. She shared that although she liked Mara a lot, there seemed to be more classroom chaos than seemed healthy, and she wasn't sure how to help anymore other than listen. Because Nancy couldn't be there during instruction time, she wondered if I might work with Mara in my role as a literacy coach.

The question was, Did Mara want to work with me?

I suggested to Nancy that I might start working with the grade level and see if Mara sought to work with me independently. After one after-school planning session working on writing, Mara invited me back to her room and talked about how much harder this job was than she had expected.

She took a deep breath, swallowed, and asked, "My principal mentioned maybe I could work on my management. Do you do that with teachers?"

16

"Constantly," I replied.

The next week I arranged an observation to get a feel for Mara as a teacher. During a short writing lesson, the noise level rose gradually. Within twenty minutes her voice matched the noise level, growing louder and louder. Then names started to go up on the board, and then check-marks next to them. Students were shushing and yelling at each other. The students with names on the board talked back. "What?! Why?" and of course, "That's not fair!"

When we debriefed, I said, "Each teacher has a different comfort level with noise and activity. Where did this lesson rate for you?"

She shrugged. "It's pretty much how it is all the time. I've gotten used to it."

"I noticed Char, Kelly, James, Zeke, Josiah, and Quinton have their names on the board, and some have checks next to them. What does that mean?"

"They miss five minutes of recess if their name is listed, and the whole recess if there is a check next to their name."

"Which rules were they breaking when they got those consequences?"

She sighed. "I don't even remember—there were too many of them."

I hesitated, and then began tentatively, "Does it seem to make a difference? When they get the consequence, do they stop the behavior?"

"They stop right then, but if you are asking if they make enduring changes, no. Those same names are up almost every day."

As we continued to talk, Mara admitted that she was missing bathroom breaks, or even any breaks at all, because she had to stay in the classroom to monitor the kids during recess.

"Are you open to considering doing something different with your rules and consequences as part of our work together?" I asked.

"If you think it might help," she said.

One Step at a Time

Management is a tricky thing for me to coach. I have to check in constantly with myself that I'm not letting my biases lead. Although there are fewer and fewer classrooms using "names on the board" systems, the classrooms I visit where kids quickly point out their "bad" peers often refer to the board. Private, not public, redirection of behavior fits my philosophy. In addition, it seems like many of the kids who struggle to fit the expectations of the classroom are kinesthetic learners: they like to move and touch and express themselves through their bodies. Yet these are the kids for whom we take away recess time?

I've spent years thinking about my teaching philosophy and honing my management style. I may be a bit of a management junkie; what works, what doesn't, and why fascinates me. I've read *Discipline with Dignity* (2008) by Curwin, Mendler, and Mendler, *The First Days of School* (2009) by Harry and Rosemary Wong, and *Nonviolent Communication* (2003) by Marshall Rosenberg, not to mention a stack of parenting books. My job was

NOT to make Mara into Heather. My job was to ask questions and create an environment for Mara to explore the causes and effects of her management choices.

Here is the work we accomplished in our first three weeks together:

Week 1
Observation and debrief; establish and reinforce a signal that means "quiet."

Week 2
Write a social contract with the class.

Week 3
Take the class through a rule a day:
- What does it look like?
- What does it sound like?
- Model and reinforce.

Philosophical Fit

At one point I asked Mara, "Does writing kids' names on the board fit with your philosophy?"

"It's what my mentor teacher used," she said.

"Sure. So of course, you would feel comfortable with the procedure. Does writing kids' names on the board feel like the right thing for you?"

She looked down. "I'm sorry how this might sound, but how else does a teacher keep track of who loses recess time?"

Through our conversation, Mara realized that she'd never questioned that losing recess time was negotiable. It's what she remembered from her experiences in school, and it's the procedure her mentor teacher had used. We discussed other consequences that would hold kids accountable for not following rules but wouldn't keep her from having a break each day and keep those kids from some necessary recess time.

As part of writing the social contract, we came up with this continuum of consequences. Mara was teaching alliteration, so she played with getting all the consequences to start with *R*:

Reminder—Everyone gets a chance to be quietly redirected.
Removal or Natural Consequences—Mara created a place in the room for kids to remove themselves from the group if they were being distracting. Other consequences would fit the broken rule.
Record—Mara had a form for students to write which rule(s) they were choosing not to follow.
Removal from Room—Mara set up a deal with Nancy that she could send kids over to Nancy's for ten minutes.
Referral—This would be a call home and/or a trip to the office for repeated issues or serious infractions.

Consistency

Over the next three weeks, Mara was tempted many times to revert to the old system. This new system felt awkward; she had to remember to use proximity with children and whisper to remind them, "Please keep your hands to yourself—this is your reminder." She also had to periodically send a student over to Nancy, her teaching colleague next door. It felt like she was admitting failure when they left the room. In the short term, yelling and missing her breaks seemed more comfortable because it was what she knew.

When she made her first call home to let a parent know about her child's behavior choices during the day, she felt sick to her stomach.

"Do I have to do this?"

"If you want to be consistent with what you set up," I said.

"I hate conflict!" she wailed.

What surprised her was that the parent was disappointed, but thanked her for caring enough to call. The parent said, "Sometimes I don't know about problems until I come in for conferences. At least now I can take Quinton's computer time away for today."

When Quinton came in the next day, there was an apology letter for Ms. Mason. His behavior improved, and he told other kids, "Ms. Mason will call your mom if you don't listen up." Quinton was fantastic advertising that the new Ms. Mason was following through on her promises.

Mara's classroom management didn't turn around overnight, but it did improve. Teacher and scholar Harry Wong reminds us that yelling and screaming are unbecoming to our profession. I agree. Mara also found that when her challenging students were getting their recess time, they seemed more able to focus on the afternoon math lesson. The whiteboard returned to being a place for recording learning instead of a chart of recess-losers.

Through my work with Mara, I got to see firsthand how hard it is to change. I experienced again the excitement of beginning a new system and how it fit her budding philosophy. Then I saw the work of maintaining it each school day, every hour, every minute. There were several steps back along the way. Management is crucial to student success. Coaching for management is a balance between sharing your own beliefs and walking with teachers as they establish their own systems and stick to them.

Consider These Questions

What kind of ongoing support is available to colleagues for management?

How do you keep from letting your biases lead?

What is negotiable for management?

What are some things that are "unbecoming to the profession" in your mind?

How can a coach support consistency?

Lesson Structure

The experts will tell you, "Add sand to water, but not water to sand" when building structures on the beach. That's because you must have a strong foundation for a sculpture that involves supersaturated sand. I know this because I've watched my husband and fellow sand men and women compete and carve on the beach. It doesn't matter if they are sculpting an octopus, a gnome, a mermaid, or a six-foot teddy bear: the foundation is key.

Though supersaturated students are not our goal, lesson structure also must have a strong foundation. We have a saying in our coaching team that "Good instruction is good instruction," meaning it doesn't matter whether we are talking tenth-grade American literature or kindergarten math; the details change, but the components of high-quality instruction in lessons stay the same.

Lesson Opener: Pound-Up

In sand terms, you begin with "pound-up." Competitors spend time shoveling sand into wooden or plastic forms to create an initial shape. A giant teddy bear would have tiers of forms to fill. About every six inches the sculptors stop and tamp or pack the sand down. Filling a form that's two feet off the ground is a different experience from propelling buckets of sand up six feet. When the sand is set, sculptors pop the forms out and get to work.

A lot of fascinating research has been done on student attention. In a rudimentary summary of a traditional lesson (mostly teacher talking) a learner's attention is highest at the beginning of a lesson. It then dips lower and lower and begins to rise again only at the end of the lesson. So lesson openers and closers are important, because students are paying the most attention. The research also shows that we have learning episodes that last about ten minutes and that if we stop and do something emotionally relevant (tell a story, show a short video, talk to someone, write), our attention perks up again, ready for another learning episode. Learning episodes for younger students are even shorter. A rule of thumb is to think of attention span as equal to the learner's age.

Let's consider pound-up at the beginning of our lesson. Eric and Allison both spend ten minutes introducing the same lesson. As you read each vignette, think to yourself, *If this is what students will mostly retain, what will they know as a result of this opener?*

Eric opens his lesson by pointing to the learning objective on the white-board, which says, *I will explain how the author uses reasons and evidence to support points in the text* (Common Core RI 4.8). He says, "So let's think about what we're going to be focused on. What's the verb?" His students respond, "Explain," and he circles it. "Today we'll be explaining out loud and in writing. And what exactly are we explaining?" His students respond, "Reasons and evidence" and he underlines them. "And for what purpose? Ah, here it is: for support. Authors know that if they want people to listen to their ideas, they need to give reasons and evidence for support. You've probably had that experience too if you wanted to stay up later. You might say, 'I went to bed early last night,' which is a reason you are giving to support staying up later. So listen up today, because improving your ability to be persuasive with reasons and evidence to support your point is an important skill in our world.

"The article that Jerry is passing out is about banning sugary-drink vending machines in schools, even the teacher's lounge. That would mean no Cokes after school. I want you to read it the first time through for comprehension of the whole thing. If you have some connections or reactions, you can jot those on the sides. Then during the second read I want you to underline softly in pencil the author's reasons and evidence to support her point about banning sugary-drink machines. This isn't about whether you agree or not—we can talk about that afterward—but it's about the reasons and evidence she provides to make her point." The students take pencils, move to reading spaces around the room, and begin reading.

Allison opens her lesson by saying, "Who remembers what we did yesterday during reading?" One student volunteers that they've been reading nonfiction. The teacher nods. "What else?" Another student says that they were underlining parts of the text. She nods again. "Why are we doing that?" Some students take guesses, and finally one says, "To underline the evidence?" Allison smiles. "That's right. We are underlining the evidence in the nonfiction text.

"How many of you drink sugary drinks?" she poses. Hands go up. "I really like Dr Pepper," the teacher says. "I like Diet Coke," says one student. "I like vanilla crème soda," says another. Several kids share their favorite drinks. "Well, today we are going to read an article that discusses banning those drinks from schools, even the teacher's lounge. So I wouldn't be able to have my Dr Pepper with lunch. How many of you think we should ban the vending machines?" Some hands go up. "We'll be underlining the author's reasons and evidence for her point to ban the drink dispensers."

Pause for a moment and consider the first ten minutes of attention span. What have the students in Eric's class focused on? What have the students in Allison's class focused on?

Eric

Students know the objective.

Students know that authors use evidence and reasons to support a point.

Students know this is a life skill.

Students know to read the article first to comprehend the piece.

Students know they are looking for reasons and evidence to support a point.

Allison

Students know what they did yesterday.

Students know they are underlining reasons.

Students know the teacher's favorite sugary drink and other kids' favorite drinks.

Students know to underline the reasons and evidence they find.

The difference between the two is that Eric is focused on using reasons and evidence to support points, whereas Allison is focused on reviewing and sharing. My point is not that we should never review and connect back to the previous lessons or get kids talking about things they like to build interest and excitement. My point is that if we have ten crucial minutes for pound-up, for setting the foundation, what is most important for learners? I contend that Eric offers clarity and focus on learning.

Lesson Episodes: Carving

I'm going to devote a relatively small amount of text to what happens in the middle of the lesson, focusing on "doing the discipline" and learning episodes.

Doing the discipline means kids are actively engaged in the verb. For example, if my kids want to learn how to carve sand sculptures like their dad, they may watch him set up the forms and help him pound up, but they need lots and lots of carving time. When we say things like "Kids don't know how to determine importance when they take notes," we need to think about giving kids lots and lots of time to determine importance while they take notes.

If kids need to shift about every ten minutes, according to that research on attention span, how can we plan that into our instruction? What would pacing look like?

> :10 Set objective, purpose, describe the what and how.
> :10 Students read article and underline reasons and evidence.
> :10 Students explain reasons and evidence out loud, begin to explain in writing.
> :10 Students reread article.
> :10 Students write exit slip on how reasons and evidence were used to make author's point.

Notice how in forty of the fifty minutes students are reading, writing, and explaining.

Lesson Closer: Sandscaping with the Primacy-Recency Effect

During the last minutes of a sand competition, tools are everywhere. Big shovels and tampers have been replaced by wedges, specially shaped spoons, cosmetic brushes, and a manually powered pneumatic sandblaster, or what most of us laypeople call straws. That's because it's time to refine, time to create those details that make spectators say, "Wow."

Being intentional at the end of a lesson is challenging. There are many days that I look up at the clock, and my carefully crafted conclusion is closed for business because we are out of time. I'm patient with myself because I know that means I was present and focused on the students. Still, I'm aware of this challenge, and I go to great lengths to set timers so that I save the last five to eight minutes of the lesson.

What do I do during that closure time? I get students actively summarizing, analyzing, evaluating, and reflecting. It might be writing an exit slip, talking with a partner, or jotting notes in a journal. I also know that the brain loves novelty, so after a lesson on reasons and evidence for informational text, I might have students choose one of four corners in the room: (1) I know how to explain reasons and evidence and could teach it to someone else; (2) I improved today in my ability to explain reasons and evidence; (3) I like explaining reasons and evidence; or (4) I don't like explaining reasons and evidence.

Closure is two-way, because I'm thinking about my three M's: Who needs **More time**, resources, scaffolding? Who has **Misconceptions**? Who is ready to **Move on**? For the students, it's a time to help them connect to what they just learned and help their brains store that information.

The primacy-recency effect as I understand it from *The Complete Presentation Skills Handbook* (2008) by Suzy Siddons describes our brains' tendency to remember what we did first and last (or most recently). Interestingly, this fits with the attention-span research that shows we'll remember the beginning of the lesson (primacy) and the end of the lesson (recency), and that the downtime in the middle is productive, thinking work but isn't captured in memory quite the same way. When we use those closing minutes to pack up, start homework, or lecture to the kids about what they just learned, we lose precious brain time.

What Do YOU Remember?

Take a moment, cover up this text, and think about what you remember. Chances are you remember the sand-sculpting analogy—how I started with pound-up to make the point about the importance of setting the foundation—and the primacy-recency effect. Here is a summary of considerations for lesson structure:

- Be intentional about opening the lesson; post and discuss the objective.

- Within ten minutes give the students an emotionally relevant transition.
- Look for students to do the discipline.
- Consider learning episodes that are ten minutes or less, to match their brains' pacing.
- Save five to eight minutes to get kids actively thinking about their learning at the end.
- During closure, reflect on the 3Ms: More time? Misconceptions? Move on?
- Then reflect: How solid is the structure of your lesson?

Virtually Coaching a Lesson

I'd been working with Chad for about two months when his first observation was scheduled. A second-grade teacher, Chad had shared with me that he didn't feel like the principal understood him. Even though he'd been teaching fifteen years, he'd had the least seniority in his grade level, so he'd been transferred to his current school the third week of September because his class size had been too small. He didn't feel he'd had time to build a relationship with the new principal, who did walk-throughs at 10:10 am, which happened to be when his class was transitioning from recess. Chad didn't feel like that made a striking impression.

The principal had asked Chad to use a specific template for his lesson write-up, and he'd attached that electronically to his email to me with the request, Will you look at this?

It's not unusual to get more requests for collaboration during observation times, and it makes sense. Teachers want an outside partner to help them think through their instruction. When I read Chad's lesson, I was glad he'd sent it and given us some time to revise it.

Don't get me wrong, there was nothing wrong with the lesson, but I knew Chad's principal well. She was the type of administrator to zoom in on, Why are you teaching this? Chad had chosen a fun book, but it wasn't clear through his description why he was doing the lesson, what big ideas and essential questions it was related to, and how he hoped it might move his students forward.

Wow/Wonder/Wow

I use the Wow/Wonder approach in feedback for kids. It's simple. Every piece of writing has something deserving of validation: a Wow. In the same way, every writer deserves the chance to grow and improve. A question prompting revision is the Wonder. The same principles work in coaching. With some adults, like Chad, I use the WWW (Wow/Wonder/Wow) sandwich. Here's why: Chad had been teaching longer than I had. At almost every meeting Chad regaled me with stories of how funny and effective he was with his students, which told me it was important to him that I view him as a good teacher. It took both courage and vulnerability for Chad to write up that lesson early and send it to me for feedback. I wanted to encourage more collaboration in the future, so it was crucial to communicate my recognition of his strengths teamed with specific, timely feedback.

In my response I told him I thought he'd chosen an engaging text for his second graders. I appreciated that he'd indicated places in the book where he was going to have them stop and talk. The Wow communicated intentionality on his behalf to think through the text and anticipate good stopping places. I wondered if the objective he'd chosen was the best fit for that particular book. He was working on inferring and was planning to have the kids predict with a popular book. "In my experience," I wrote in the email, "it's hard to have kids predict when several have read the book. Do you think that might be an issue with your students?" My wonder was checking in on the match between text and purpose. Then I went on to validate that he'd tied independent writing into his lesson with the reading. The second Wow ended the communication on a positive. I also knew he'd been trying to incorporate more writing so it was also validation of his growth.

What Should I Do?

Chad responded after school. He wrote, "Because you mentioned the point about kids having read the book, as the kids were leaving I asked them how many of them had read *I Know an Old Lady Who Swallowed Fly Guy* by Tedd Arnold and they told me the librarian had read it to them! That would've been a disaster. What should I do though? My observation is Thursday."

I picked up the phone and called Chad. I shared with him that unusual or off-the-beaten-path books often prove best for predicting. "And predicting isn't just about thinking 'what's going to happen next' in my mind. It goes with other comprehension strategies too."

"I've never really thought about it that way. What other strategies does it pair with?" Chad asked.

I shared with him a recent lesson I'd taught using *The Aminal* (2005) by Lorna Balian with first graders. "It's a story reminiscent of the telephone game, where there is an animal, and as each child tells about it, the Aminal gets bigger and more dangerous. It naturally invites predicting, but if you hide the illustrations, it has great language that also invites kids to visualize."

"Do you have the book?" he asked tentatively. I scooted back in my chair and found it on my bookshelf. On his way home from school, he stopped by my office and picked it up.

The Power of a Smiley Face

Chad read the book that night and rewrote his lesson with a clearer understanding of how this specific book could help kids deepen their inferring skills. He sent the revised lesson to me on Wednesday. With the WWW sandwich, I shared what worked, gave him one question to consider further about how it would connect to future lessons, and then told him I thought it would go smashingly.

During lunch on Thursday, Chad emailed to say that his principal had taken copious notes during the lesson, laughed aloud with the kids as they shared their thinking, and left a smiley face sticky note on top of his observation notes. As we'd discussed, the kids wrote throughout the lesson and the principal asked him to bring the students' writing to the postconference so she could make copies of it. To her, it symbolized the important ways that reading and writing go together.

Collaborating with Principals

Even though the principal and I never spoke about Chad's observation, we were collaborating. Her purpose was to evaluate Chad, and my purpose was to use the evaluation as the focus for a professional conversation. The experience provided a unique opportunity for Chad to open the door to coaching and receive feedback before a formal observation. Because he'd made revisions that he deemed successful, he was motivated to collaborate with me again. It was a win for me in that I strengthened trust with a colleague, a win for the principal in getting to see Chad in a new light, and best of all, a win for Chad and his students.

Consider These Questions

What sorts of coaching requests do you get?

Will you look at this?

Have you used some form of the WWW sandwich? How does it work?

When giving feedback on a lesson for observation, what parameters do you consider?

How to Use
a Coach

When my husband and I rented the movie *Slumdog Millionaire* (2008), I hid my eyes frequently during the first thirty minutes. Completely unprepared for the onscreen violence, I asked Kurt to nudge me when the torture sequences were over. In particular, there is a scene where two criminals cover up a young orphan boy's mouth with a rag soaked in an etherlike substance. I knew something terrible was about to happen.

I paused the film and told my husband, "I know this movie won awards, but I can't handle this." He agreed about the intensity, and we turned it off.

The next night my friend Beth, who happens to be a life coach, was over for dinner. I told her how hard the first half hour was and said, "Tell me a reason to keep watching."

"Actually, what happens after that scene is where the movie shifts completely and gives you the first breath of hope. Do you want me to tell you what happens to the boy?" I nodded and listened. After she left, we were able to finish watching the movie, and I understood why it came highly recommended. I was happy I had hung in there.

What does this have to do with coaching? Well, I needed a lifeline. I needed someone who had seen and heard what I hadn't to let me know what to expect, to let me know there was hope ahead. I needed someone who listened and said, "The first thirty minutes were hard for me too." Beth wasn't a *Slumdog Millionaire* expert, but she knew enough to move me forward.

In the same way, I'm not an expert in the classrooms I enter, but I often know enough to help a teacher move forward. As an instructional coach, I've worked with first-year teachers, a thirty-two-year veteran, and many stages in between. Some teachers seem instantly comfortable with the coaching arrangement, whereas others (because of apprehension, misinformation, or just being new to the process) need to learn "how to use a coach" to their advantage through the process.

Purpose

One of the questions I often ask in my initial meeting with a teacher is, What do you already know about coaching? Our principals have been wonderful in getting the word out about the value of coaching, but even some of the best-intentioned have said to their teachers, "So if you have any problems, we'll get you connected with a coach." It's true we love to problem-solve with teachers, but you don't have to be in a slump to benefit from working with a coach.

Tracy Gregorius, a seasoned primary teacher, described her experience being coached. "The misconception that I had before beginning is that teachers need the coaching because they are struggling in an area of their instruction. I also didn't think that coaching would involve modeling lessons if I wished. In the past, I saw other teachers coming in to teach your students as a sign of being not so good at your job."

A good instructional coach will share the purpose of coaching and the vision the district has for teacher collaboration. Teachers tell me they are relieved when I share the purpose of coaching and restate many times and in many ways, We believe that *all* teachers deserve coaches.

Before coaching, Paul Johnson, a fourth-grade teacher, had a concept of more directed coaching. "I guess I expected that I would just be told how to do things instead of actually being able to watch and collaborate to build a series of lessons," he said.

Leah Workman, a second-year teacher, echoed that idea. "When my coach first came in, I was anticipating that she would assess and let me know what I needed to work on. Instead we talked about my frustrations and put together a plan of action around my concerns, not hers. The coaching model was very much teacher led."

Model

Once we have the purpose and vision established, we can get more specific: What does coaching look like? Does the coach observe? In the front of the room or back? Does he or she take notes by hand or on a computer? Will the teacher see those notes? What kind of feedback does a coach give? Is the coach open to modeling lessons? What kind? What does the teacher do during the lessons? What about coteaching? Does the coach predetermine the focus or does the teacher, or some combination of the two?

After we discuss why I observe, I often get this question: What if my lesson bombs? I respond, "Then I will recognize myself in you, because I have had many lessons bomb. In fact, that's why I'm a coach—because I've been there and had to figure out what's next. Plus, I may have something not go so well when I'm teaching too, and I need permission for that to be OK." We talk about how when students aren't showing evidence of what we thought they knew or what we thought they could do, it just gives us information about what we need to think about for tomorrow. Coaching is a continuous process.

Confidentiality

At the risk of sounding like a health teacher during a talk about puberty, it is "perfectly normal" for teachers to worry about being judged. In fact, I haven't worked with a teacher yet who hasn't mentioned it at some point in our coaching cycle. Teaching is personal. We share who we are through our teaching, and some of us have had very little outside feedback about this dance we do each day with our students.

Open to the work, but still feeling hesitant, Leah Workman shares, "When I was approached to work with a coach, I had two thoughts. The first was, That sounds comforting since it's my first year without an adviser or mentor. The second was, I don't want to be judged. I was concerned before the first meeting, because inviting someone back in to observe me seemed like I was taking steps backward."

Becky Lee, an experienced teacher, concurred. "At first it is intimidating to have another professional come to your room. You don't want to be judged, and it brings up all your old insecurities about what you're doing that isn't good enough. Although you know the person is coming in to support you and serve as another set of eyes, you can't help but feel a little trepidation. Is it safe to show this person what I don't know?"

I still remember a very traditional teacher asking me, "How do I know, even with your pledge of confidentiality, that you won't go tell my principal or your colleagues about how 'old school' I am and how much I need a new set of batteries?"

I smiled and said, "Because you've been around long enough to know that if I did that, the rumor mill in this district would start up in no time. It would get back to you, and you would tell everyone, 'Don't ever work with that coach,' and my job would be over." She returned my smile and said, "You're right. Let's get to work."

If coaching is optional in your school or district, it is absolutely acceptable to ask a coach for a reference. Several teachers have admitted to me that they didn't return my phone call or email before they had checked with another teacher I'd worked with to make sure it was worth their time. I'm not offended by that; it's a smart use of time before making a commitment.

Clarity

The teachers who have put me to work most efficiently spent time thinking about what they wanted to get out of coaching. They have clarity around their curiosity.

In our first meeting I heard specific requests such as these:

"I'm worried about the amount of teacher talk I'm doing. Can you give me feedback on it as you observe?"

"Because two-thirds of my students are boys, I'm concerned that the girls never volunteer and always wait to be called on. I'd like your perspective on that."

"The class as a whole is great, but I don't seem to be able to motivate Andrea, Byron, and Cheri, and I want new ideas."

As educators, we sometimes proceed with a mile-wide focus, when what we really need are small steps to go deep. Still, if a teacher is unsure about what small steps he or she could be making, that will become clear through the work. I appreciate teachers who say, "I'm unclear on what I want to work on; I just know I'm willing to do the work." Having clarity around a lack of clarity is good information too.

I sometimes joke that the initial meeting can feel a little intimidating, like being the new kid on the playground and walking up to a peer, saying, "Do you want to play?" The teacher and I ask questions and offer our stories to build a connection. It's all about relationships, and coaching is no different. The opening conversations take place in library corners, at kidney-shaped reading tables with books, and even at coffee shops. When we begin by taking time to discuss purpose, the model, confidentiality, and clarity, the foundations have been strong for our work together.

Recapping: Four Things to Consider

1. *Ask about the purpose of coaching.* If it's not stated or printed, ask, "What does the district or principal envision as the goal of coaching?"
2. *Ask about the model.* If the coach doesn't walk you through what it can look like, ask for specifics.
3. *Share your concerns openly, ask about confidentiality, and if possible get references.* It's perfectly normal to wonder what's in it for you and your students. I am secretly thrilled when teachers ask for this information, because it lets me off the hook and gives someone else the opportunity to talk about what coaching has meant to him or her.
4. *Get clarity on your curiosity.* You've been given a gift of another set of eyes, ears, and hands. Think about how your students can benefit most from this opportunity.

There are additional practical pieces that help a coach get to know you and your class, such as having a copy of your class list available along with your social contract and schedule.

Just as "one size does not fit all" in teaching, the same is true for coaching. An instructional coach is not an expert on your teaching or your students; he or she strives to use observation, feedback, research in best practice, and reflection to walk with you on this journey of improving student learning.

As Tracy Gregorius puts it so well, "As teachers every summer we say, 'Next year I'm going to. . . ,' and September rolls around and we hit the ground running. Often we never go back to those thoughts or changes we wanted to make in our instruction. Having a coach work with you can make those 'summer wishes' become a reality."

To Be of Use

I've used mnemonics for studying since I was in middle school. Funny, easy-to-remember phrases, raps, and poems triggered associations to Spanish words, parts of a cell, and later, psychoanalytical theories of development. In fact, my mnemonics were so good, my husband outscored me on the Abnormal Psychology midterm; his only test prep was mnemonic prep the night before the test. Using this learning aid, I created "Peppers Make Cats Cry" to help me remember the components I want to communicate as a coach during my initial meeting with a teacher. Because I can picture little kitties sniffling about spicy jalapenos, I'm able to keep in mind the four things I consider important.

Peppers Stands for *Purpose*

A friend of mine goes to networking meetings for her business, and they open the meeting with each entrepreneur's thirty-second pitch. It got me to thinking, *Could I share the purpose of coaching in my district in thirty seconds or less?*

Although it changes depending on my listener, I want to make sure I communicate the vision of my work: "I collaborate with teachers in professional development as well as in their classrooms to improve student learning through effective use of curriculum and instruction."

As we set the purpose, I want to know about a teacher's background and experience with coaching. When I ask, "What do you already know about coaching?" I frequently hear, "Very little." Their responses also echo myths that coaching is only for beginning or struggling teachers. Sharing with teachers a "This I Believe" reveals my intention, and they appreciate the repetition of my mantra, "I believe all teachers deserve coaches."

Make Stands for *Model*

A few teachers are ready to dive right into coaching without much thought of what lies ahead, but most teachers appreciate a little preview of the journey. During my first year of coaching, I used a short video I created with another teacher to show clips of how each step might look. In other situations when that seemed too formal, I drew a circle and labeled each step as I talked about the process.

Often our first step after the initial meeting is to observe. I like to spend about twenty minutes with my laptop or notepad to transcribe the classroom interaction. Twenty minutes seems to be about right, so I get the feel of the classroom culture without having too much information to process during the debrief. The transcribed notes are nonevaluative, to the point that I tell the teacher that students can walk behind me and see I'm typing a script of what kids are saying and doing. Before the observation, the teacher and I establish something for me to "watch for" so I can give helpful feedback on his or her instruction. Sometimes it is as broad as "classroom management" and sometimes it is as narrow as "Pay attention to Patricia and Luis—I don't think they are being challenged enough." After the lesson, as soon as possible, we debrief. I give the teacher a copy of the transcript and we read it aloud to give our conversation context.

During that debrief we'll determine the next step. For example, a teacher who wanted me to watch for classroom management, Pam, mentioned that there were long chunks of teacher talk in her transcript. Pam wondered aloud how she might get the kids to interact more with the material. I asked her how much experience she'd had with cooperative learning, and she said, "Not much. I mostly hear that feedback from my principal, like, 'You could use more cooperative learning,' but I really don't know how to do that other than have them sit together." It was clear that demonstrating a lesson with her content and her students would be meaningful for her so she could see cooperative learning in action.

Chris, a fifth-grade teacher, asked me to look at his students Patricia and Luis because they were so far ahead of the rest of the group. As we debriefed, we saw the need to compact the curriculum for these two. Our next meeting was a planning meeting, and then we cotaught a lesson so that he could get the class going on an activity. Then together we introduced an independent learning contract to Patricia and Luis.

My "coach key" might look like this with a teacher like Pam. If the teacher answers yes to the question, we move on to the next step.

> **Initial Meeting:** Is the teacher willing to have me observe?
> **Observation and Debrief:** Would the teacher find it meaningful to see the strategy demonstrated?
> **Demonstration Lesson and Teacher Observation:** Does the teacher want some guided practice to try on the strategy?
> **Coteaching and Debrief:** Does the teacher want to see the model again as he or she is giving the new strategy a go?

With Pam there was more demonstration up front with gradual release; she took on the strategy herself as she was comfortable. Chris, in a much different place and ready to take on complex differentiation, wanted more planning and coteaching up front. Although they took slightly different paths, both teachers used student data and observation to make decisions, focused on research-based information, and reflected on the process.

Cry Stands for *Confidentiality*

Until my fifth year of teaching when I had a student teacher, the adults in my room observing my teaching consisted of the principal, paraeducators, parent helpers, practicum students, and the teacher of our buddy readers. All of those educators were there to evaluate, support, or learn from my teaching—no one had ever been in solely to give me feedback to improve student learning. This is why I completely understand how foreign it is when I introduce the coaching purpose and model. Even the very best teachers share with me that they wondered in the back of their minds, Is she going to judge me? After all this time, what if I really don't know what I think I know? Am I working with a coach because I'm struggling?

At every initial meeting, I make sure to say, "My notes and feedback are for you and you alone. If you choose to share them with colleagues or your principal, that's great. I will tell your supervisor only what we are focused on and when we are working together." At this point many teachers wave me off and say, "I'm not worried about that." I make sure to add, "It's important for me to share that with you, because coaching is about information, not evaluation, and I don't want you to have any concerns. I want us to have space and time to experiment and make mistakes and focus on our work for the kids' sake."

Cats **Stand for** *Clarity*

My family members and I are the adoptive parents of three guinea pigs. Cooey, Rascal, and Rocket are adorable—and messy. As they speed around their cage clucking, "Wheep, wheep, wheep," they kick out aspen chips that line the tray. I am constantly picking up and sweeping while the other four members of the household walk by without noticing or, frankly, caring about the wood chips on the floor. That's how we are with teaching too: there are things we pay attention to and things we don't. Over time, I've found it is a waste of my time and energy to give feedback about wood chips when wood chips don't concern the teacher. Instead more investigation on my part is required.

The first time I ask for clarity is in our initial meeting when I ask a teacher what he or she would like me to "watch for." If a teacher has been very specific in answering the question, What seems to get in your way of teaching at times? I may already have my "watch-fors." Here's a sample of an interaction with a teacher I'll call Edna:

Coach: What seems to get in your way of teaching at times?
Teacher: My students aren't independent at anything. They can't even write a complete sentence.
Coach: When you say that about complete sentences, about what percentage of your class are we talking about?
Teacher: I'd say seventy-five percent.
Coach: That's intense for fifth grade, isn't it? About eighteen of your students are not constructing sentences. What are they writing?
Teacher: Oh, they are writing, all right, but there isn't any structure to it—no organization, no capitals, no periods.
Coach: Do they like to write?
Teacher: They hate it! They groan at ten thirty [writing time].

This teacher has given me a lot of information in this brief exchange. First of all, it's likely that Edna views good writing as conventionally correct writing and thinks three-quarters of her class are below standard. It's possible that there is so much focus on complete sentences that kids have stopped enjoying and exploring the other traits of writing. They hate writing and she hates writing—whew!

Here is how I might suggest what I could watch for: "You mentioned all the kids who aren't writing complete sentences. What if, during my observation, I watch for all the ways that the other twenty-five percent are engaged in writing and we can work from there?"

If I gave Edna the message that editing was the least of her problems, she might not be invested in the next steps of the coaching cycle. Using a strengths-based approach means that when Edna sees kids more excited about writing at ten thirty and more effort toward writing correct (and engaging) sentences, she's going to feel better about what's happening in her classroom. Along the way there are other huge shifts happening in the writing process focused on content. Over time and with trust, Edna and I can engage in conversation about complete sentences inside the deeper inquiry of "What is high quality writing and how do you teach it?" When I get clarity on where Edna is and how she sees her class, I start there.

Changes in focus are common in coaching. A teacher had specifically asked me to watch for how students were using "good reading behaviors" during her lesson. During our debrief I was being shadowed by another coach whose mouth dropped open when the teacher said in reflection, "I really just want to get my students to prewrite better. Can you model that next time?" What happened to the good reading behaviors? The observation served the important purpose of helping her get clear on what she didn't need: feedback on good reading behaviors. We could then focus on what she did need: more confidence with how to get kids started writing.

Peppers Make Cats Cry

At the end of my initial meeting with a teacher, I look over my notes and check off the following items: Did I mention the purpose of coaching? Did we discuss the flexible model? Did I share the confidentiality clause? Does the teacher have clarity on what he or she wants to get out of the work, or will that come later? I don't really know if peppers make cats cry, but I do know that when those four components—purpose, model, confidentiality, and clarity—are in place, we have a strong foundation upon which to build our coaching relationships.

Consider These Questions

What is your purpose for coaching or mentoring? What is your model? How does confidentiality and clarity play into your work?
What are important components of initial meetings with teachers?
    Are there ones you would add or delete from this short take?
Which coaching questions that you ask seem to give you a lot of
    information?

Best Practice All Day Long

Engaging Problem Solvers: Math Literacy

A second-grade collaborating teacher was working on the standard of composing and decomposing numbers and wanted to create a rich problem-solving task to look at the strategies students were using to solve problems. After studying several tasks online, we co-created this one to connect to a recent field trip to the Pumpkin Farm.

We need to bring back eighteen pumpkins from the field. Each bag can hold two pumpkins, and each wheelbarrow can hold three pumpkins. How many bags and wheelbarrows will we need to bring in the pumpkins?
Show your thinking in words, pictures, and numbers.

When constructing a problem-solving task, we attempted to balance engagement and personal connections without making it so engaging that students departed from the math. After the field trip, I read the task to the children and a second grader's hand shot up. "I think that every student should just carry their own pumpkin so we don't even have to figure this out," she said.

I chuckled. "OK. So let's imagine we are bringing back extras for other people at school."

"Who gets the extra pumpkins?" the children wanted to know.

Once we had safely navigated back to the pumpkin problem and away from whether Custodian Dan would get one or not, some students drew quick sketches of pumpkins while others counted out eighteen Unifix cubes. Some counted by twos, some counted by threes. One student started with a bag, then a wheelbarrow, then a bag, then a wheelbarrow, got to seventeen, and then asked, "If I just have one more pumpkin, couldn't I leave it there?"

I prompted, "What else could you do?"

By the next day, the teacher and I were looking over her students' work. They'd drawn accurate, labeled pictures, and their equations were satisfactory, but their explanations in writing needed some work.

One wrote, "I got 9 bags because that's how I knowed how to do it."

Others included more text; for example, "I got 3 bags and 4 wheelbarrows. Squish! That's me at the muddy pumpkin farm. I really like pumpkins. The big ones are the best. I hope you like my words!"

The teacher said, "They are either writing something that tells us nothing about how they solved it or they are writing a lot that doesn't have to do with math."

Mathematician Marilyn Burns says in her book *Writing in Math Class*, "When solving problems, students should be required not only to present answers but also to explain their reasoning. I tell children that their papers should convince the reader that their solutions are correct and also reveal how the students arrived at their solutions" (Burns 1995, 69).

Choosing Mentor Texts

Together we decided that a good place to start was having the children rank three sample papers from weakest to strongest so we might use the strongest paper to record attributes of good math writing. We created our own mentor texts based on what we were seeing as a proficient student's writing (Text 3) and some nonproficient students' writing (Texts 1 and 2).

Text 1: Elaboration, but not about math

I did the math problem. I got 9 bags or 6 wheelbarrows for the 18 pumpkins. I drew pictures of the pumpkins. I didn't put faces on them. Most of the pumpkins were big because I like the big ones. It was hard to draw the wheelbarrows. They looked more like cars. I also wrote an equation for my pumpkins.

Text 2: No elaboration

The Pumpkin Farm has lots of pumpkins. A bag can carry two. A wheelbarrow can carry three. I would take 9 bags that's how I know how to do it.

Text 3: Our model

This problem is called the Pumpkin Problem. First I knew I had 18 pumpkins to bring in from the field. I drew the pumpkins in twos because I knew that two could go in a bag
$2 + 2 + 2 + 2 + 2 + 2 + 2 + 2 + 2 = 18$. Then I got 9 bags. I also saw I could get another answer so I drew the pumpkins in groups of three because I knew three could go in a wheelbarrow
$3 + 3 + 3 + 3 + 3 + 3 = 18$. Next I got 6 wheelbarrows. It makes sense there are more bags than wheelbarrows because wheelbarrows can hold more. Finally, I knew that I could use 9 bags or 6 wheelbarrows, and maybe there are even more answers.

All but four students agreed that Text 3 was the strongest. They were getting the idea. Here is our anchor chart of what the math writer was doing well:

- Names the problem
- Tells the steps in the right order
- Uses transition words such as to begin, next, then, also, finally
- Explains the math thinking
- Tells the answer and explains why it makes sense

Sentences Like Buddies

With the model to work from, students were sequencing the steps about *how* they solved the problem, but we weren't getting into the *why*.

How could we encourage these seven-year-old writers to include more details in a concrete way? I thought about a recent primary lesson where I'd taught students that sentences like to have buddies. During that lesson, I'd had all the students say the name of a buddy out loud.

"Amir!" "Maria!" "Lucy!" "Fletcher!" "Daisy, my dog!" they called.

"Most of the time," I said, showing them a sketch of Calvin and Hobbes, "we are better off with a buddy than without. Sentences are like that too."

I had them lift a line from their journals. Just one. "Now consider what a reader might wonder, and write a buddy to go with the sentence to tell more," I said.

Lifted line from a student's journal: "Mrs. K lost her voice this week."

Reader might wonder: What was that like?

Student's buddy sentence: "She talked so quiet that we had to come up close and fold our ears open."

Transferring a Writing Strategy to Math Writing

"What about having them use buddy sentences in their math writing too?" I proposed. We discussed how using a tool from their writing workshop would be powerful for them when writing in the content area. Our new problem-solving task was similar to the pumpkin problem in design:

> *Twenty-four kids want to go sledding down a big hill. Circle sliders can carry two kids. Rectangle sleds can carry five kids. How many different ways can the 24 kids sled down the hill?*
> *Show your thinking in words, pictures, and numbers.*

After I was certain the students understood what the problem was asking, I released them to work on it. As their pictures, numbers, and equations appeared, I had them talk to a partner about their strategies.

Then I wrote, "This problem is called the Sled Problem."

"What do you wonder as readers?" I asked.

One student piped up, "What's it about?"

"OK," I said, "so I'll add a buddy." I wrote, "24 kids need to sled down the hill in circle sliders or rectangle sliders."

"What else should I tell?" I asked.

"What you did on your paper," one said. "Like first I . . ."

I wrote, "First I drew 24 kids and circled them by twos."

The kids said, "Add a buddy! Add a buddy!"

I wrote, "Each of the circles showed one circle slider . . ."

There is a limit to how much elaboration is desired in math writing. After all, one of the attributes of high-quality math writing is succinct, to-the-point, no-frills writing. Once writers are past the point of "This is the answer" or "I just knew it," they'll study math writing and learn the specific type of "how" elaboration that is appropriate when writing to learn.

Scaffolding for Young Writers

When kids write in math, they learn to present their ideas effectively and don't stop with, "I just knew it." A number of steps can help teachers scaffold the way to students' independence in math writing.

1. Create and share three or more mentor texts that reflect the kids' approximations as well as a model of proficient writing for the grade level. Have the students discuss and rank them.
2. Record the attributes of the strongest piece. This can be turned into a checklist.
3. Model the use of buddy sentences to encourage elaboration of why students chose their strategies and procedures.
4. Share a student-friendly rubric so students know what the expectations are.
5. Give plenty of time and feedback for writing.
6. Finally, think about how often we publish students' poems, artwork, and stories. Publication tells kids, "This is important. You are a writer." Doesn't content writing deserve the same attention?

Consider publishing students' math writing in a variety of ways:

- Send it as a letter to families—i.e., "This is how I solved my problem."
- Send the problem to another class at the same grade level and then exchange writing to see how they solved it.
- Publish it on the bulletin board.
- Create a class book.

Recently I worked with a second grader who was reluctant to write about math. I asked him, "Who do you care about? Let's pretend like we are explaining to that person."

He said, "I care about my dad, and he's in Afghanistan. I couldn't even show him this unless I sent it to him."

"Great idea," I said, and at the completion of the project, we sent an electronic package of kids' math writing more than 6,000 miles away.

Consider These Questions

What is your resource for rich problem-solving tasks?

What models do students see of math writing?

In your mind, how much elaboration should there be in math?

How is content-area writing honored in your classroom and school?

Math, Writing, and Coaching to Learn

In *Writing to Learn* William Zinsser says, "Writing is a way to work yourself into a subject and make it your own" (Zinsser 1988, 16).

I get many invitations to collaborate in writing instruction and work with teachers on problem solving in math, but it's rare that I get an email that combines both like Lisa's: "I'd like to do some procedural writing in math. Can we collaborate on that?"

I immediately found a block of days so we could "work ourselves" into math through writing.

Lisa, like many intermediate teachers, works in a departmentalized arrangement. She begins the day with her homeroom kids, and then about every eighty minutes she rotates through three different groups of fifth graders for literacy. Excited about learning more about writing in the content areas, she wondered what connections she might build with other members of her teaching team. When we sat down to plan our work, I asked Lisa about her goals for the students with this project.

"I want them to understand what procedural writing is, and how it's different from the creative writing we've been doing. And I want them to like it and not be bored by it," she said.

"Sure," I said. "And by *different*, what do you mean?"

"Well, catchy leads aren't important with the procedural piece, and word choice is—but in a different way, because they should be using math vocabulary."

Lisa's thoughtful request about liking it and not being bored by it is an important consideration. Marilyn Burns, in *Writing in Math Class*, says, "I think that some students resist writing for one of two reasons. They either don't see the purpose of the writing assignment, or they're uncomfortable with what they're expected to write and don't want to be unsuccessful" (Burns 1995, 185).

Purpose

When I think of the word *purpose*, my former student Alex comes to mind. Early in the year I told my students, "If you don't see the point of what we are doing in class, I want you to challenge me and say, 'Mrs. Rader, what's the purpose of this activity? How will it help me as a learner?'" Well, Alex didn't see the point of much of anything in my class—besides lunch and recess—so he'd raise his hand and challenge me: "What's the purpose of this?" I learned to anticipate and appreciate these challenges; he was actually giving me the opportunity to restate the learning objective and make a connection to the kids' real-world experiences.

To communicate the purpose of math writing, Lisa decided to hook the kids with the procedure of making a peanut butter and honey sandwich (which is her typical after-school snack). Following the students' verbal directions, she made the point that you can't skip steps and that the words you choose are very important.

One student said, "Now put the peanut butter on the bread."

Lisa set the jar of peanut butter on the two slices of bread.

"No!" said the student, laughing. "You have to open the peanut butter, get a knife, and spread it."

Lisa feigned surprise. "Oh . . ." She opened the peanut butter, got a knife, and spread the knife around inside the jar.

"No!" a girl took over. "You have to get a dollop of peanut butter on there."

Lisa stopped, looked confused, and asked, "What is a dollop?"

"It's like a spoonful," she said. "Maybe a tablespoon or two."

At this point, I chimed in, "That's what we are talking about with procedural writing. You have to get down the small steps and not just jump from the bread to the peanut butter spreading. As far as word choice goes, we are looking for very precise words so everyone knows what we mean. *Tablespoon* is an important word choice in this case."

Shared Understanding of Writing Instruction

During planning I asked Lisa, "How much support do you think the students will need?"

"Since they haven't done a lot of this type of writing before, I think they'll need a lot of support," Lisa said.

"How about creating a model and then using shared writing?" I suggested. Lisa nodded.

At this point I paused, because I was thinking about how we throw terms around in education with very different understandings of meaning. I've watched a "guided reading" lesson that was round-robin reading, and I'd recently been invited to see a "shared writing" lesson by a teacher doing all the writing and thinking—there was nothing "shared" about it.

I work hard to make sure the teachers I work with and I are using terms and their meanings in the same way by checking in about our vocabulary. As Lisa and I talked, my yellow pad zipped out and I sketched a continuum while I did a think-aloud. "When I think about writing instruction, I think about four types: modeled writing, shared writing, guided writing, and independent writing."

- Modeled Writing
- Shared Writing
- Guided Writing
- Independent Writing

"If your students had had many experiences with nonfiction writing in math and science, we could probably start with a more guided approach, but since they are new to it, we need to start here." I drew an *X* on the *modeled* and *shared* writing portions of the paper.

Then we clustered our associations for each of the terms to build common language:

> modeled writing: all teacher
> shared writing: mostly teacher and the students contribute ideas
> guided writing: students now hold the pencil and teacher provides
>   support
> independent writing: students in control of writing

Debriefing

Over a few days of our coteaching, the students "worked themselves into" math through procedural writing. After three weeks of being in her classroom, Lisa and I developed a problem-solving task called the Window Problem that would draw on students' knowledge of area and perimeter. Because of the reality of our busy schedules, she and I had an electronic debrief.

Heather: What about procedural writing was difficult for your students?
Lisa: It was difficult for my kids to identify the steps that they took in solving the problem. They knew what things to do, but couldn't always see that there were multiple steps involved. In their minds, you do what you do and that's it. For example, although it may have made sense for them to draw a picture of the window before finding the area and perimeter, they didn't see this as a "step," but rather as something that just made sense to do. As a result, the write-up was challenging. There were large chunks missing that they didn't realize were necessary to include.
Heather: What supports that we put in place were helpful?
Lisa: It helped some to show the example of making a peanut butter and honey sandwich where leaving steps out could be disastrous. Still, even though the effect of leaving out steps was clear, some still did it anyway. The shared writing piece was huge in getting students to correct this, because they were able to think through the steps together and listen to us as the teachers doing a think-aloud. It was really nice when you'd say, "Wait, no . . . that's the peanut butter—I need the bread!" and they made that connection.

Here are some reflective questions an instructional coach might ask of a teacher:

> What do you want this project to teach students about being a
>   writer?
> What may be/was difficult for the students?
> What supports will we/did we have in place for the difficulties?
> Now when you say X, do you mean . . .?
> What comes to mind when I use the term _____?

Here are some reflective questions about writing in math for coaches to ask themselves:

> Where do we see examples of procedural text in real life?
> How might students connect and engage with the content best?
> What terms might you be using with teachers that would benefit
>   from some clarification?
> What do you do for teachers who learn visually and kinesthetically
>   during your planning sessions?

Bringing the Outside In: High-Quality Science Observations

In her third-grade classroom, Debbie Davis-Reid and I were observing students the first few days of writing workshop, inspired by Ralph Fletcher and Joann Portalupi's *Writing Workshop: The Essential Guide* (2001) guiding questions. Who starts quickly? Who adds to their authority list? Who takes time to get something down? Who says, "I am a writer" and who does not?

An authority list is something unique to every "author." A list of people, places and things that the writer is on good authority to share.

One student I'll call Kaleb wrote on his authority list after ten minutes: *I do not like to write. I like sines. I love sines outside. Sines in nature. Sines by the water.*

I bent over and said, "Tell me about this word," pointing to the word *sines*, unsure whether it was *signs* or *science*.

"I love science. Mrs. Davis-Reid is really into science too," he said.

"I find it interesting that you don't like to write but you love science, because those two things go right together." He shrugged.

During our debrief, Debbie and I noted five kids who didn't seem to be generating their own inspired ideas yet. With those students on my mind the next morning, I spotted a huge dirty onion in our home pantry that smelled like spicy earth. I grabbed it by its greens and headed to Debbie's school.

Moments before the students came in to start their morning routine, Debbie and I planned to invite Kaleb to explore some science writing with the onion if he seemed interested.

As if on cue, Kaleb walked in, said, "Good morning," and looked right past me to the table where the monstrous onion was waiting for him.

"What," he said, throwing down his backpack, "is that?"

I told him that if he was interested, because he was so into science, he might have the onion on his desk during writing workshop and show some of the other students how to make observations in writing as a scientist.

"I could do that," he said, straightening his shoulders.

Kaleb wrote a few inspired lines that day, and so did the girls sitting next to him. When we shared their observations under the document camera, Debbie posed, "How many of you think you might like to write some observations?" About half the class raised their hands, including the other four who hadn't been enthusiastic for writing workshop yet.

Backyard in the Classroom

The next day I let out a "whoa" when I saw Debbie's back table covered with ferns, fungus growing on bark, and vines with berries. The kids responded the same way, and couldn't wait for workshop time.

After a safety talk about never using our sense of taste with scientific observations and always washing hands at the end, Debbie placed the backyard forest items around the room, and kids congregated with their notebooks. For the first five minutes all they did was talk. "Look at this! It's shaped like a nose!" and "I poked this berry with my pencil and it looks like it has blood inside," and "There is a pincher bug!"

Debbie came over and we had a quick conference. "They aren't writing," she whispered.

"I know," I replied, "but their talk is all observation. Let's give them some more time. Maybe I'll write under the document camera."

I placed my notebook under the document camera and started writing about Kaleb's onion. I peeled off the skin and looked through it. *Did you know onion skin resembles college-ruled paper?* To this observation I added, *I wonder how many layers make up an onion.*

Ten minutes in, about half the class had picked up their notebooks to record their observations. The noise and excitement faded to calm focus. Within fifteen minutes, Debbie and I beamed at each other. They were all writing!

Concrete, Representational, Abstract in Writing

"How can I have this be part of the workshop on a regular basis," Debbie wondered, "and have it be more manageable?"

We talked about incorporating "pick-up" items on the science table. What if during workshop there were natural items available that writers could bring back to their writing spot? It reminded me of how I have samples of student work, teacher quotes, and sticky notes of the brilliant things kids say sprinkled all over my workspace. They are the pick-up items that form and inspire my writing.

In math we think about moving students from the concrete to the representational to the abstract. The same can be true with writing. Students begin with a concrete item that they describe and discuss, move to the representational with a picture and labels in their notebooks, and then move to the abstract: a piece of science writing.

To scaffold high-quality observation writing, I introduced Debbie to *My Nature Notebook* (2008) by Kevin Beals, part of the Seeds of Science, Roots of Reading series, which models a studentlike observation of the natural world over time and comes with a strategy guide to teach what makes a high-quality observation.

In Debbie's workshop some kids are writing fantasy stories, some are writing personal narratives, and some now have observations adjacent to berry stains.

Often teachers ask me, "How do you know that next thing to hook particular kids?" I suppose in this case Kaleb himself told us what was next; we just read the "sines."

Consider These Questions

What do you find when you interview seemingly reluctant writers?
What models of observation writing do you have available for students?
Do you work with writers like Kaleb? How do you hook them?

What Velcro Can Do: Coaching in Science

"You aren't going to be the science program police, are you?" Donna asked when I asked where science fit into her day with fourth graders.

"No, I'm not the science police, but are kids really not doing any science?"

"You know my schedule. I don't have any time, and I hate having my room be a mess."

That's true. Donna had explained from the very beginning how it was going to be: "I like boxes and labels and everything having a place."

I was about to say, "But good learning *is* messy," but chose instead to listen to Donna and begin within her parameters: no science kit, no mess, and it had to fit in her schedule.

At home that night I was reviewing the picture book *Marvelous Mattie: How Margaret E. Knight Became an Inventor* (2006) by Emily Arnold McCully to use in my professional development with a narrative summarizing strategy. Never again will I think about the paper bags at the grocery store in the same way. I loved the book because it tells a story about perseverance and resiliency. If something doesn't work, you just try it again and again and again.

Kind of like teaching. Kind of like coaching.

I Googled the word *inventions*, thinking that I could hook students into this book by sharing some background information about inventions. Reading about inventions led me to a site that talked about things that were discovered by accident. One of those inventions was Velcro. George de Mestral, I was fascinated to read, got the idea for Velcro after taking a walk with his dog and returning to find burrs attached to his wool socks.

Even though it was pushing 11:00 pm, I went rummaging around in my sewing box and pulled out two swatches of Velcro. Peering closely, I studied the loops on the soft side and the hooks on the grippy side. As the mother of three little ones, I'd always been thankful for Velcro, but I'd never stopped during my please-hurry-up-and-get-your-shoes-on-we-are-going-to-be-late speech to notice the wonder of it. My natural curiosity started up. What if thin tissue was inserted: would it be unable to hook? Does Velcro work if the loops are wet? Why does Velcro eventually wear down—because the loops break or because the hooks relax? Or both?

As I was just drifting off to sleep, an "aha" popped into my consciousness. Not only was *Marvelous Mattie* going to be marvelous for my professional development with teachers, but Velcro was going to help me hook Donna into doing science!

Curriculum Police

Donna is not the first one to ask me if I'm going to police her curriculum. As teachers define what "coaching" is for themselves, they ask these types of challenging questions. In our district, there are nonnegotiables such as learning standards and then there is curriculum provided to support those standards. Teachers have choices to make about how they use the curriculum to make the standards come to life. Because I work with the standards in many classrooms, I know the variety of approaches teachers take—some more effective than others. But my title is "instructional specialist," not "curriculum specialist," so I focus on effective instruction for student learning no matter what the curriculum is. Still, Donna was choosing not to use the science materials and instead had held on to outdated textbooks written above students' comprehension level and focused on small details and vocabulary out of context.

I decided that it was Donna's principal's job to talk with her about whether to use science kits. If her principal was in her classroom frequently and knew the standards it would become clear that instead of a science kit exploration table, there were old green science books. All the principal needed to do was ask the same question I had: When and how are your students doing science? Even though it was hard for me to imagine why a teacher would not want to use a well-designed system for scientific exploration, it was my job to work with Donna in a different approach that could help the scientific process come to life in her classroom. The point is for students to engage in scientific thinking, and there are many ways to get there.

If/Then

If I could start right where Donna was, *then* we had a chance of moving toward having students develop a conceptual understanding of what it means to "do science" as a scientist.

That was my hypothesis.

I had three consecutive days planned in Donna's class during her forty-five-minute writing time. As a believer that writing can happen in every subject, every day, I asked Donna if the two of us could plan writing in science for those three days.

"There will be no mess," I assured her, "and I will bring everything in a labeled box." She smiled.

I brought along my Velcro swatches and told her about my discovery. My idea was that we'd spend the first day with the students, exploring the Velcro, drawing and labeling pictures of the two different sides, and doing some observation writing. Donna made her own self-to-Velcro connection when she talked about how her children were young in the late seventies/early eighties and how much more independent they felt when they fastened their own shoes.

As Donna and I looked at the student work from the first day, she marveled at the accuracy of their drawings and the great connections in their observations. One student wrote, "It's like when you make your hands into C-shapes and then connect them and pull. It's very strong." Another student wrote, "Now I know why burrs stick to my dog!"

The second day was the If/Then writing day. This was the day I would suggest that scientists often begin with a question and a hypothesis. We would provide them with some other materials and have them design their own mini-experiments (that were not messy) in pairs. When one of the pairs had the same question as I had—What happens if Velcro is put in water?—Donna found a plastic pipette (that I'm pretty sure was from one of the science kits) and a cup of water so they could find out. That pair wrote, "If we put water on the soft side, then I think the Velcro will still stick because Velcro can go through the washer and dryer but it might not stick as well."

On the last day, they shared what they had observed with each other and wrote a brief conclusion. I did a short minilesson about how conclusions may or may not be in agreement with your original hypothesis and that that's good science.

Donna asked the students, "Does this remind you of what we are talking about right now in reading? How we drew conclusions about our character, but they weren't always in agreement with our predictions?"

"Absolutely," I said. "It's the same idea."

My Conclusion

Making connections between science and reading seems to be an "in" for me with many teachers. If they can see that the cognitive processes in reading instruction are the same but look a little different in science, they feel more comfortable. Frankly, I don't know how science got this bad rap for being messy and taking over classrooms. It's true that can happen, and I'm in some amazing classrooms where it does. But it doesn't have to. Thinking scientifically can happen with magnets, paper airplanes, leaves from the playground, and even the Velcro on kids' shoes. The important part is that it happens.

Through coaching, I know I built a trusting relationship with Donna. I know that we engaged the students in writing and science as real writers and scientists. We saw evidence of their thinking through student writing. I know that Donna's "aha" when she saw the connection between reading and science and realized that science doesn't have to be huge and overwhelming was important. What happens now is up to her. I have propped open the door for Donna so that when she's ready to engage in more science, I am right there to roll up my sleeves and work with her. Maybe her principal will ask her to open up that science kit and she'll contact me begrudgingly at first. Maybe she'll come to it on her own. My final words to her were "All you have to do is ask," because that is what a scientist would do.

Consider These Questions

Do you ever feel like the curriculum police?

What is your comfort with connecting reading and writing to science?

What is a current "If/Then" hypothesis in your work?

Social Studies: Keep It Current

While student teaching, I was invited to a teacher's classroom on a Thursday for Current and Cocoa. By the sink, kids scooped Nestle Hot Cocoa mix into their personal mugs, added hot water, and then meandered to the carpet with scraps of news. The teacher read for a short time from a news article she'd clipped and then shared her thoughts. Any kids who chose the same article could read a different section and/or respond with their thinking. We heard about car accidents, politics, celebrity news, and sports that day.

This is what living the study of the social is all about, I thought. Civics, economics, geography, and history had been my least favorite classes in school because they were distilled to names, dates, and meaningless details. Social studies connected to my life only in the sense that I had to commit facts to short-term memory so I could get an A in the class.

But Current and Cocoa was something else entirely.

Starting Conversations

Paul Johnson, a fifth-grade teacher in my district, invites each student to bring in a news article to class meeting time once a week.

He says, "It's important because it is a way for the kids to make connections to and develop opinions about world events. As the year went on, often kids would say, 'Whoa, that's like x or y that happened earlier this year.' Or, 'That makes me sad, just like x made me sad in December because . . .' Simply having a candid, free-flowing discussion about the news inspires kids to think, dream, and see themselves as part of this massively complex world."

As a beginning teacher I had the notion that to orchestrate grand conversations in social studies, I had to have deep content knowledge. And that's true to some extent; I have much to learn. But it's also true that simply by living an examined life, I do have content knowledge. I know enough to start a conversation about our "massively complex world."

Managing

Management strategies for communicating in a large group are key to the success of sharing circles. Paul said, "The most difficult part is keeping the conversation going. This got much better throughout the year as we worked on communication/listening strategies in our literature circles. For example, we discussed adding on to someone's point, agreeing and disagreeing with a 'because' statement. The stovepipe effect is in full force during News time because they are so excited to share what they saw or heard that they have a tendency to blurt out random events rather than making a connection with what someone else said."

Paul requires the students to choose one news event each week and record it on a news form by quoting from or summarizing it. He acts as the facilitator, filling in knowledge when it's needed, defining words when he can, and mostly supporting the kids to talk to each other and stay on topic—at least for a little while. I recently had the opportunity to transcribe in his fifth-grade room.

A "News" Session

Teacher briefly reviews expectations.

Teacher: Remember, if you have something to say, you can just say it. Wait if someone else is talking, but you can join the conversation. While you are waiting to share your news, set your papers down so we don't have crinkle, crinkle, crinkle.

Student: There were a hundred and sixty tornadoes that destroyed houses in Alabama.

Teacher: Where did you find that?

Student: Online.

Teacher: Who has something that connects to that story?

[*Student reads story about rescuers who had to leave the dead.*]

Teacher: Other thoughts or connections?

Student: I feel sad that they had to leave the dead.

[*Several kids nod solemnly.*]

Student: The tornadoes are caused by wind currents.

Student: It's also affecting cows.

Teacher: What do you mean by that?

Student: All sicknesses go through the udder into the milk, so Japan is affecting lots of things.

Teacher: Remember that Japan's struggles with the tsunami were due to an earthquake, which is a different situation than the weather. I'm curious to go back to the tornado thing. How did you know about the wind currents?

Student: From the video we saw—you know, my schema.

Student: I read that there were a hundred and thirty-one people killed, but the hospital wasn't damaged, so they were still able to treat people.

Student: That's cool that the hospital wasn't hurt at all!

[*Kids start talking excitedly.*]

Student: About the wind currents, it's like what Gina said, you know, when it's hot first and then a cold front hits it and it makes a supercell, like a waterspout.

Teacher: So you are backing up to the wind current we saw the Brain-
POP video about how the air starts spinning, but you said something
about hot air and a cold front.

Student: Yes, the air is hot first, and then a cold front comes in.

Teacher: What is a cold front?

Student: I don't know because it confused me.

Student: Like rain? Thunderstorms?

Teacher: A cold front is the front of weather coming—the leading edge—
and it takes the place of warm air. Just so you are clear, that doesn't
always make a tornado. That's more likely to happen in the center of
the country. It's not impossible for one to happen here, but it's un-
likely.

Less than five minutes of talk and grand conversations abounded in the
circle. To begin, there was a misconception that Japan's tsunami was
caused by wind. The teacher addressed it and continued to keep kids on
the topic at hand. Then there was an opportunity to define a cold front.
The teacher helped the students understand that they were making connections between what was happening in the news and a video on wind
they'd watched in science. Most important, children felt and expressed empathy for Southerners they'd never met.

In the last few minutes of the sharing time, a student shared an article
about a Superman plaque that was cut off a post in Cleveland. The author
of the story predicted that the thieves either planned to use the bronze or
sell the plaque as Superman memorabilia, which moved the students to
consider ethics.

Teacher: If you buy something stolen, is that OK?

Student: If you don't know that they stole it, then how could you know?

Student: I don't know. It makes me think of the video we watched.

Teacher: Right. After reading *Becoming Naomi Leon* we watched the trial
of the stolen radio, but the defendant was claiming that he didn't
know. The jury determined it wasn't OK, and you voted and determined it wasn't OK either. If something is too good to be true, you
need to listen to your instincts, and trust yourself. I think trusting
our instincts is something to pay attention to.

Student: What if my instincts are telling me that I want to eat a pig?

Teacher: Then you must be hungry. Let's wrap it up.

[*Students laugh.*]

What's Essential?

It's been a long time since my exposure to Current and Cocoa days through
student teaching, but it was wonderful to revisit my belief that news is essential curriculum. Here are some tips to make the "study of the social"
doable in classrooms:

Create a sacred sharing time every week.

Revisit the protocols for the meeting often.

Model, model, model about how to discuss news.

Use the same form week after week that includes a place to record where the news was captured (such as a website, newspaper, radio, or television program) and a summary and/or quotes from the story.

Know that attention spans are shorter in the beginning and that you need to work slowly toward building listening stamina.

Teach conversation skills one at a time and in context. For example, use one week to teach students how to connect to another's story, and follow it with a week when you focus on how to question a classmate.

Trust yourself to have enough background knowledge to facilitate conversation. Remember that the opportunity to say, "I don't know; let's find out about that" is a great model for lifelong learning.

Although my initial experiences with social studies weren't engaging or relevant to my life, I've found a new respect for the discipline through mentors and colleagues. I know it can be different. As Peter Johnston says in his book *Choice Words*, "Pressures of testing and overstuffed curricula easily make us abandon meaningfulness and reduce our view of our work to mere individual cognitive skill building. It is easy to forget the need to engage the whole person in joint community activities that are socially and personally meaningful and emotionally satisfying" (Johnston 2004, 73).

Consider These Questions

What was your experience as a student of social studies?

What needs to be in place for the talk to flow so that you can have deep conversations with students about current events?

What might you add to "what's essential"?

Where have you seen meaningfulness reduced to skill building?

Coaching
Social Studies

Social studies is one of the few subjects that has no statewide assessments tied to it. The upside is that many teachers enjoy social studies autonomy, and the downside is that many teachers employ social studies obscurity (the quality of being unknown). In response to new legislation in civics education, I piloted a class with fifth-grade teachers. Our purpose was to prepare and, by the end of class, write, our own classroom-based assessment essay as teachers. I chose the "You Decide" assessment and this topic: *Should violent video games be considered free speech and be protected by the First Amendment?* In this exploration we would state our opinion on a public issue, provide background on stakeholders' positions, and explain how a right or common good connects to the issue. We would use our own learning experience to build a future unit for the students. It was particularly timely since a local boy had suffocated as a result of his friends burying him headfirst in a sandbox. The boys were mimicking a character in the popular video game Naruto, in which the objective is to reduce the opponent's health to zero.

Throughout the classroom-based assessment course the teachers and I had many "aha" moments about our lacking civics education. As hard as it was, we realized how important the work was. In a democratic society, we can't just teach kids how to read articles and give their opinions so they can vote one day. We need to teach them how to gather information, listen to the law, listen to reason, compromise, collaborate, and ultimately understand how informed decisions affect us all.

After completing the class, a teacher whom I'll call Marla asked if I would come work with her in her classroom as she implemented her first classroom-based assessment. She had majored in history in college, so she felt comfortable with the civics aspect, but she wanted my help with the reading and writing components. I was excited. We decided to focus on "Whose Rules?" a similarly constructed civics classroom-based assessment that asks the students to "identify a problem and a policy or law that attempts to solve it." We chose to focus on seat-belt laws. We knew this was something opinionated fifth graders could access.

Skills Wanted

It was a Tuesday, and Marla invited me in to watch the kids set up their notes on the first stakeholder: the Safety Restraint Coalition. The task was to provide information about how this organization had participated in the lawmaking process. Marla had done a great job of selecting text that the kids could comprehend and of providing definitions for words such as *restraint, manufacturer,* and *citation.* Walking them through the notetaking process became a focused, intentional lesson, and the kids were enjoying themselves.

Two days later I was back and Marla assigned students a short practice write in which to use their notes and write about the role of the Safety Restraint Coalition in the lawmaking process. While they ate lunch, we looked over the student work.

"It's like they've never written before," Marla moaned.

We considered the three types of student writing: verbatim sentences from notes (most), opinion-only writing (many), and explaining the purpose of a seat belt (two). I asked, "Do kids know how to use paraphrasing, quoting, and summarizing?"

"Apparently not, from looking at these," said Marla.

As we moved into the "what to do" phase of our conversation, we brainstormed a list for paraphrasing, quoting, and summarizing. Alongside our sandwiches, Marla and I noted that the purpose was the same for all three strategies of information sharing. We talked about how we as adults decide when to paraphrase, quote, or summarize.

Paraphrasing Nonfiction
- Purpose: Share information without altering the meaning of the original text
- Source: Needs to be cited
- When do we use it? When our reader would appreciate us putting it in our own words.

Quoting Nonfiction
- Purpose: Share information without altering the meaning of the original text
- Source: Needs to be cited
- When do we use it? When the source is well known and/or credible. We may choose quotes when they are technical, catchy, or very important in their original form.

Summarizing Nonfiction
- Purpose: Share information without altering the meaning of the original text
- Source: Needs to be cited
- When do we use it? When we can select or write a sentence or sentences that capture the author's most important and repeated ideas.

Through the discussion, we narrowed our instructional focus to paraphrasing and quoting, because Marla's fifth graders had spent several weeks on summarization of nonfiction text. Marla said she was going to review summarization and asked me if I would model how to quote and paraphrase from the Safety Coalition text.

To Quote or Not to Quote

While modeling the think-aloud strategy, I wanted to make it clear that although there was no definitive right or wrong, some information was a better fit for quoting and other information was better suited to paraphrasing. I read this Safety Coalition statement and asked the students to consider quoting or paraphrasing.

> *Placing a child in the back seat instead of the front seat reduces the risk of death by 27 percent. (http://www.800bucklup.org/laws/index.asp)*

One of the students said, "Well, it just makes sense that you would quote that one."

"Why does that make sense?" I asked.

"That's their whole point . . . that it's safer and it just says it."

"True," I said, "so a simple sentence that is a very important point is a good one to quote."

A few days later students redid the assignment and we saw beginning evidence of the strategies of paraphrasing, quoting, and summarization.

TAPC©

Then Marla said, "OK, so what about citing?"

When I was a teacher-librarian, I came up with the acronym TAPC© (pronounced tap-ka) to capture the five parts needed for most citations:

T itle
A uthor/s
P ublisher (or publishing site for electronic sources)
C ity of publication (or URL for electronic sources)
© copyright (or date site was accessed for electronic sources)

We began incorporating TAPC© into our note-taking sessions. Because we were using both printed book and electronic resources, we had a great opportunity to show the kids how to gather the same information from different places. This became the template for our citing expectations for the final product of the classroom-based assessment.

Reflecting

Marla started off her reflection at the end of our coaching cycle by saying, "At first I was wondering how the classroom-based assessment was going to take as much time as you were planning, but then as we got into it, I realized how many sub-skills we needed to teach kids to help them toward independence. In the past, I think I would've been frustrated with their early attempts and thought it wasn't possible. I'm going to be able to use those lessons on quoting and paraphrasing in all different areas now, and TAPC© is stuck in my head for good."

Consider These Questions

When you look at enduring work in social studies, what underlying sub-skills might students need?

When you write information from nonfiction text, do you (as a writer) use paraphrasing, quoting, or summarizing most?

How do you decide when to use one or the other?

What ways can you help make citing sources accessible to students so that it just becomes "what we do"?

Same Difference

Have you ever wondered how two similar movies can be released simultaneously? Take *A Bug's Life* (1998) and *Antz* (1998), for example—both animated insect movies with misfit ant heroes overcoming adversity and winning the affection of the princess. Or *Megamind* (2010) and *Despicable Me* (2010), both with minions (which now appear prolifically in students' writing) and freeze rays. While Mega and Despicable are unique superheroes, the plots revolve around the bad guy transforming into the good guy. Coincidence? I think not! Perhaps it begins over a power lunch with two or more creative folks and someone says, "What if we step into the insect world and take an ant and make him the protagonist . . ." Then they each go off to their separate studios and create the stories that emerge as fraternal twin movies.

The tendency for our brains to take in information during a movie or any other time and say, "Oh, that's like . . ." and "That's different from . . ." helps us understand how each brain is wired differently. We store and chunk information based on experiences. The more personal connections we make to a concept, the better we can remember and use the information.

Similarities and Differences

As we acquire knowledge, we are constantly categorizing what something is and what it is not; in short, we are thinking about similarities and differences. In *A Handbook for Classroom Instruction That Works* (2004) by Robert J. Marzano et al., there are four related categories: comparing, classifying, creating metaphors, and creating analogies. In the meta-analysis work done by the researchers (studies upon studies), they determined that explicitly teaching students to find similarities and differences is one of the most effective high-yield strategies.

When I *compared* the movies *Megamind* and *Despicable Me*, I was examining how they were alike and different based on their characteristics. If I were to give you a list of movies, you might be able to classify them by grouping those with similar characteristics. Metaphors are two very different things that share some similarities. Students wrestle to find commonalities when I say, "A sponge is a summary." A step beyond metaphors, analogies look at relationships between pairs.

Comparing

Joyful Noise: Poems for Two Voices (1988) by Paul Fleischman is a lovely book for fluency and expression, but it also provides an engaging model for kids to compare and share. My initial model acted as the hook to engage kids and discuss the purpose of comparing.

I am Megamind.
I have a big blue head.
My minion is a fish.
My nemesis is Tighten.

I am Gru.
I have a long nose.
My minions are yellow.
My nemesis is Vector.

We are really bad guys
who hatch evil plans,
and we both have minions.

In the end, we turned out
to be good guys after all.

I invited two students to read with expression and be Megamind or Gru. Afterward, I shared with the students how the similarities came through both voices and the differences by each individual reader. The students brainstormed pairs of words that could be compared and talked in partners about similarities and differences. I then provided them with a blank organizer to draft a short poem for two voices. One pair created this about their favorite animals:

I am the turtle.
I have a hard shell.
I eat grass and leaves.
I can hide in my shell.

I am the bear.
I can roar at people.
I eat meat.
I can go in a cave or den.

We both swim.

We can both bite.

Now that the students had practiced comparing and sharing, we could use the same approach to study geometric figures, inherited versus acquired characteristics, nouns and verbs—you name it. It is especially effective with two topics that students often tend to confuse with each other.

Creating Metaphors

A fourth-grade teacher said her students were having difficulty keeping narrative and expository writing straight. Although they could list the attributes of each one, they often couldn't tell them apart by the term alone. This was a great place to use a metaphor, especially because the students had been studying the two concepts for some time. Here's how I began the lesson to create metaphors for narrative and expository writing:

"If I said to you, 'Mrs. Jones is a walking computer,' would I mean that she has a keyboard for teeth and a monitor for a face?"

The kids chuckled.

"No. What might I mean?"

"That she has a lot of information?" one student started.

"That you can ask her anything and she'll know how to find it?" another tried.

"That's great. You are all thinking of ways that Mrs. Jones is a computer. That's what metaphors help us do. We take something quite different from Mrs. Jones—a computer—and then we explore the characteristics they share. Today we are going to take all the things you know about narrative and expository writing and create some metaphors to deepen our thinking about them."

They reviewed the anchor chart of some attributes of narrative and expository writing.

Narrative:
- Means to narrate
- Write to tell a story
- Has a beginning, middle, end
- Could be a real or imaginary story
- Usually has story elements
- "Three Little Pigs" is an example of narrative text.

Expository:
- Expose, or explain in words
- Has a main idea and details
- Has a catchy lead and satisfying conclusion
- Found in many of our nonfiction books, but you could also explain something imaginary
- *Time for Kids* articles are an example of expository text.

We brainstormed a list of unrelated objects such as an ant, a DVD, a hot dog, a cat, a pillow, a pencil, a coffee mug, and a teddy bear. Together we attempted shared metaphors.

"How might narratives be an ant?"

Students turned and talked, making both close and wild associations.

As we came back together, one said, "Ants live in hills, and sometimes our papers pile up over there." He gestured to the turn-in box, and the kids laughed.

Another said, "Ants have three body parts and so do narratives, like beginning, middle, and end."

With several examples under our belts, I had the kids work on their own or in partners to create metaphors. Here were some that they authored:

- Narrative writing is my uncle because he is a storyteller.
- Narrative writing is an ant because it has a beginning, middle, and end.
- Expository writing is About (dot) com because its job is to explain.
- Expository writing is my football coach because he's always explaining (yelling about) what I did wrong.

Summing-Up Strategies

Focusing on similarities and differences is well worth instructional time as students construct knowledge about new, difficult, or confusing concepts.

Whether I'm encouraging students to compare, classify, create metaphors, or draw analogies, I'm using these components of instruction:

1. Begin with an engaging model. Show kids what it looks like outside of school subjects.
2. Try one together.
3. Offer an organizer to support their attempts.
4. Offer guidance as they "approximate" what it should look like.

With any of these activities for discerning similarities and differences, I anticipate that students' responses will be somewhat shallow at first. Many of the associations can be very superficial, such as *the ants live in hills* and *the papers pile up*. This relationship doesn't really help students understand more about narratives because all papers can pile up; it's not specific enough, but it is a start. The more practice students get, the deeper they go. The same student who came up with the anthill later came up with the football-coach metaphor for expository writing (which excited many of the students who loved football in that class). Coincidence? I think not.

Consider These Questions

Taking into consideration your grade-level standards, what are some of the topics and concepts that are new, difficult, or confusing for your students?

Which ones would be a good fit for comparing, classifying, creating a metaphor, or analogies?

What are all the ways in which students explore similarities and differences? Where do you see those represented?

How might these same activities work in adult professional development?

Ubiquitous Venns: Coaching for Depth

You see them everywhere, those friendly overlapping circles. Some are hand-drawn and look more elliptical than circular, and the intersection is never large enough for all the shared attributes to fit.

Val was using Venn diagrams when I slipped into her classroom. She'd emailed me the previous day, asking me to listen for clarity in her directions during reading. Lately, she'd said, she felt like she was constantly interrupting the kids to add clarifications to her directions, and she wanted to be more clear the first time around. She read a highly anticipated section of *Frindle* (1996) by Andrew Clements and then turned to her large chart paper, where she had written the characters' names. Nick Allen's name on one side and Mrs. Granger's on the other.

fifth grader

funny

goofs around

Nick Allen

red curly hair

distracts teachers

fifth grader teacher

strict

older

glasses

Mrs. Granger

stubborn

white hair in a bun

works hard

teaching a long time

The kids began to list characteristics for Nick—*fifth grader, red curly hair, goofs around, distracts teachers, funny*—and for Mrs. Granger—*strict, white hair in a bun, fifth grade teacher, teaching for a long time, older, works hard*. And for both? It was a stretch, but one student contributed, "They both have glasses," and another student said, "Stubborn."

Val's directions were clear. The students were to compare themselves with either Nick Allen or Mrs. Granger. They received a blank Venn diagram and went to work. Their student work was at the same level of the example. Most of the attributes were gathered from the illustrations or direct statements about the characters.

When My Watch-For Is Not My Leverage Point

After the lesson, I shared my observations about Val's directions: my "watch-for." She had modeled the expectations, explained in simple language, had a student paraphrase directions to check for understanding, and asked, "What are your questions?" before releasing the kids. The kids did exactly what they were asked; the directions were stellar.

However, my mind was noodling on something else entirely. Noodling is my husband's word to describe what is happening when he is thinking deeply and quietly about something. He uses it at times to say, "Let me noodle that up for you." So noodling as I was, I was thinking about my own leverage point. By leverage point I mean the instructional or management focus that will lead to improved student learning for that lesson and others to follow. I first learned to identify leverage points with Katherine Casey, coach and consultant, via her book, *Literacy Coaching: The Essentials* (2006).

Val had asked me to watch for the clarity of her directions, but my leverage point would've been to deepen the students' thinking around character traits. It wasn't difficult for them to look at pictures and recall stated traits. The purpose for using a Venn diagram, and in fact to study similarities and differences at all, is to go deeply into attributes or traits: to think, to infer, to conjecture, to challenge.

But Val didn't ask me about that.

I listened and waited to see if there would be an opening, and it came when she asked, "Is there something else that you might suggest? The kids did what I asked, but I guess I thought it fell a little flat."

"When you say 'fell flat,' what do you mean?" I asked.

"Well, it just didn't seem like the rich activity I wanted it to be."

Yes! That was it! *Frindle* is a fabulous book to use when discussing the nature of learning, of words, of community. Nick Allen and Mrs. Granger are rich, complex characters, and they have a lot in common. They both love language, and they both use it to better their world.

What If?

"In another classroom I'm working in, I saw a Venn diagram that was focused solely on character traits," I said. "I wonder if focusing the comparing on character traits would mean you get less of the attributes like 'curly red hair' that came from the cover picture and more deep thinking about the characters." I paused.

"Maybe that's what I meant by 'fell flat,'" Val said. "They just seemed to be sticking to the easy stuff—you know, the stuff that anyone could see. We've been working on inferring, and I hoped that would come through in this work."

Together we sketched out another Venn diagram that went deeper. We used words about how Mrs. Granger was commanding and Nick was accustomed to being the center of attention, and how they were similar. We anticipated some kid-friendly words to talk about that.

"And then we need our evidence, right?" I said. "Both of us agree that Nick likes to be the center of attention, and we could find sentences in the text that back that up."

Val said, "I think a lot of my students think anything goes because they don't have to back it up with evidence. And I didn't do that in my model, so they didn't know to go there."

Reflection

Moving from clarity in directions to providing evidence and a laserlike focus on thinking resulted because Val gave me an "in" and was open to reflection. When I use the "what-if" strategy in coaching, I simply introduce a different direction in the lesson that may change the outcome. It's not a judgment on what would've gone better. Val is the expert on these students and on her teaching. It's simply a "what-if" that can provide the next step to reflection. In Val's case, it provided her with her next day's lesson. She was excited to share her thinking with the kids and to add the piece that asks, "What's your evidence?"

Consider These Questions

How do you see Venn diagrams used in the classrooms in which you work?

What do you think about "less is more" related to Venn diagrams?

What strategies do you use when the teacher's watch-for (what he or she is interested in getting feedback about in the lesson) is different from your leverage point (the instructional or management change that may affect student learning)?

Helping Children Build Notetaking Skills

When I was a college student, I was a paid notetaker. I shudder now to think of the poor students who reviewed my laborious notes. Possibly the sole qualifications for that position were the ability to meet deadlines and legible handwriting. Because there was no requirement that one be able to actually take effective notes, I ended up in the course Dinosaurs 101 with my handy-dandy notepad, ready to make ten dollars a class. The professor was a mere speck on the stage behind the podium, but when he started speaking, I knew that the note subscribers and I were in trouble.

In the first ten minutes Professasaurus Rex (as I nicknamed him) rattled off fifty dinosaur names that I could not identify, pronounce, or spell, with no visuals to help. My single notetaking skill was to write as fast as I could and try to get everything down, which is why the note subscribers got short novels of notes for every class. I only hope they lined their pet cages with them, because I can't imagine the notes were useful for anything else.

Not Naturally Notetakers

Effective notetaking involves a writer making meaning with his or her notes by distinguishing what is absolutely essential to know, good to know, and nice to know. In other words, good notetaking involves thinking and decision making. Verbatim notetaking is the least effective way to take notes (for more information on note taking, I recommend *Classroom Instruction that Works: Research-Based Strategies for Increasing Student Achievement* [2001] by Robert J. Marzano, Debra J. Pickering, and Jane E. Pollock.) I discovered this firsthand when I gave a preassessment to first through sixth graders as a teacher librarian.

"Take notes," I instructed them, "in the way that is best for you."

The younger students took notes about tigers and the intermediate students took notes about roller coasters, but the results were essentially the same: almost every student quickly wrote down as much as he or she could. Some wrote notes in a cluster, and others wrote them as prose, but they still tried to get as much information as they possibly could onto the page.

At the next staff meeting I showed the notes to teachers, and they were surprised. "But I have been teaching two-column notes since September," one fourth-grade teacher exclaimed. "Not one of them used two-column notes!"

When teachers listed all the forms that they give students to take notes, it began to make sense. Students could successfully take notes on a graphic organizer in the context of an assigned project, but they weren't transferring the skills. Taking notes was something they did for *that* teacher or *that* project—not for themselves.

I wanted to find a way to take notes that allowed students to learn to make their own organizers and use the notes to make meaning. One successful approach that I've taught for years is combination notes.

Combination Notes

"What do you expect to get on a combination pizza?" I ask students as I start my note-taking lesson.

"Pepperoni!" "Sausage!" "Onions!"

"Anchovies!" And then every student says, "Ewww," even though some have never tasted anchovies or may not even know what they are.

"Yes," I say. "*Combination* means more than one topping on the pizza. So when I say *combination notes*, you can think of more than one part that goes into the notes."

I have students take a piece of paper—blank or lined—and fold over the right third to make a crease (that's about as wide as four kid fingers with the thumb tucked in). Then they fold up the bottom about the length of one thumb and crease the page. To finish, they label each of the sections:

Words	Pictures
Summary	

Important to Note

Combination notes are a takeoff on Cornell notes used in college and have solid roots in brain science. In combination notes, students represent an idea, fact, or event in a few words on the left side, and then symbolically represent it in pictures on the right side. Our brains like to be dually stimulated as we make meaning. In addition, there is the summary space provided to focus in on what is most important. This space encourages writers to revisit and revise our notes as we go.

I like to use Lila Prap's book *Why?* (2005) as I teach primary students how to use combination notes. For example, as I open to the passage on zebras, I read it aloud the first time so that kids can hear it in its entirety.

"'Every zebra has a different and unique stripe pattern, just as every person has a different and unique fingerprint. Their stripes can be used to tell them apart, but many scientists believe their stripes also help confuse predators'" (Prap 2005, 4).

"What's this about?" I start.

"Zebras," they say.

"What about zebras?" I say.

"About their stripes."

I then do a think-aloud of what is important to keep, and explain how I limit my words. Each time I record something in words, I move over to the right column and draw a representation.

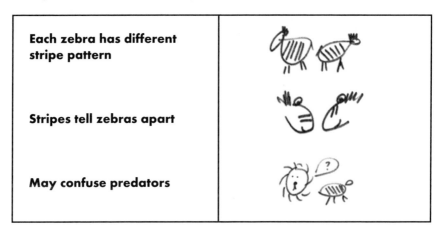

Each zebra has different stripe pattern	
Stripes tell zebras apart	
May confuse predators	

I point out that my representations just need to make sense to me, and demonstrate how I spend about twenty seconds on each quick sketch. Zebra portraits can come at another time.

"Why didn't I include something about the human fingerprint?" I ask.

"Because that was just a catchy lead," a second grader says. "It's not a fact about the zebra stripes." I enjoy hearing language from their writing workshop enter into the discussion, and realize that most of the time we don't take notes on catchy leads. Leads have an important, but very different, purpose.

Who Teaches Notetaking?

I was meeting with a team of intermediate teachers to select a reading and writing strategy to support comprehension of nonfiction texts. One teacher ruled out notes. She explained, "They really don't need that skill until middle school. I know teachers do a lot with notetaking then."

As a parent, I was surprised to see an F among a column of A grades during a middle school progress conference for one of my children. The teacher saw me eyeing it and said, "Oh yes, many students failed the notetaking pretest. They try to write everything down verbatim instead of breaking information down into chunks."

"Who teaches students how to take effective notes?" I asked.

"That is a skill they learn in elementary school," she said.

Both teachers are right. We need to be teaching students how to take notes in elementary schools, and we need to be teaching notetaking skills in upper grades too. As text gets more difficult and notetakers have a variety of structures to choose from, they need support to customize their notes in a way that helps them remember and review information.

Putting It All Together

The research on notetaking says that a variety of structures (cluster notes, combination notes, two-column notes, three-column notes, and more) can be effective when students make meaning and actually *use* their notes. Reviewing and revising notes plays into how notetaking affects achievement positively, which is where the bottom box for summary in the combination notes comes in.

With primary students in the zebra example, I discuss, model, and use shared writing for the summary. My summary reads, "Stripes help tell zebras apart and may also help confuse predators." As students get older, I gradually release the summary statement to them with explicit instruction.

Just imagine if you had left an empty box at the bottom of your college notes and at the end of each day, took the time to reread them and write a simple statement summarizing what was important in them. In this scenario, you would have returned a few times to those summary statements and made revisions as you learned more. In a class focused on big ideas and concepts, those bottom-line summary statements could have been a very powerful study tool. I can only imagine what I might have gotten out of Dinosaurs 101!

Consider These Questions

What is your style of notetaking?
How do you use notetaking in your life?
Is there vertical alignment through the grades for notetaking?
How do you explicitly teach notetaking?
How do you scaffold the use of and revision of notes?

Reflecting with Transcripts and Word Clouds

When a colleague shared the word cloud generator at Wordle (www.wordle.net) with me, I was intrigued. I pasted in quotes, poems, lyrics, and biographical blurbs and found an entirely new way of looking at words. Wordle increases the font size of a word based on frequency. For example in a song with a great deal of repetition like "We Wish You a Merry Christmas," the words *We all want some figgy pudding* would be three times larger than *a cup of good cheer*. Inputting a transcript from a presentation of mine, I laughed when the word *so* was larger than most other words. It's true. I am a so-er. It's my equivalent of *umm* and helps me transition as I think of what I'm going to say next. So. . . with transmitting language to text in mind, I was curious about what would happen if I pasted in transcripts from the teachers I was working with. What would Wordle out?

Note: There are other word cloud generators besides Wordle, such as Tagxedo and Tagul. Search for "word cloud" and choose the one that works best for you.

Magnification

I decided to take a transcript from a beginning teacher and another one from a more experienced teacher (student names were changed, though not the repetition). Even more synchronous was the fact that both the writing lessons were at the same grade level.

Take a moment and consider. Which one came from the early-career teacher? What are your assumptions that lead you to your selection? What do you know about your own journey as an educator?

What was magnified for me in Figure 6 is the reactive management language (i.e., I'm *waiting*). Most of the repeated words were commands or students' names. Maribeth? Maribeth? The few content words that appear are less specific.

In Figure 7, I see evidence of proactive management and language of the discipline of writing: *details, exaggeration, strong verbs, drafts,* and *revise.*

74

Figure 6

Figure 7

Were your assumptions correct? The first sample is from an early-career teacher, and the second is from a more experienced teacher. However, there are many teachers all along the experience continuum who could represent Figures 6 and 7. What we can see through the word cloud is that one teacher's language is focused tightly on content and using specific vocabulary, and the other's language is focused on corrective management. If what we say in the classroom and what we repeat is what gets reinforced, what did the students in each of these lessons learn? If we included only student language, what parallels might we see?

Transcripts from Coaching Conversations

As I became interested in looking at my language as a teacher during my coteaching and demonstration lessons, I also started to think about my language as an instructional coach. Recently, as part of the work in my coaching professional-learning community, I took my small video camera and pointed it at myself during a conversation I had with a first-year teacher about conferences. The next day, I sat with my laptop while the video played, transcribing my questions and the gist of her answers.

I reflected on how coming into the conference, I had seven resources on the topic of conferencing in my coaching binder. In my first year of coaching, I would've handed all the resources over, but now I know to use my questioning to distill what might be truly useful to each teacher.

For example I asked, "How much do you want the kids to be leading and how much do you want to be leading?"

She explained that she would be leading the conference and that students would chime in about some pieces of their work. The article that I'd brought on student-led conferences would not be of interest to this teacher.

I probed for how much she was going to do proactively with the kids to set them up for success with questions such as, "As they are sharing their work, are you going to do any practice beforehand with that? Or will it be in the moment?"

More than halfway through the conference, I asked, "When you think about conferences, what are you most nervous about?" and the conversation shifted. She shared that she was nervous about not being able to anticipate what the parents were going to be concerned about. Being on the spot with an inquiring parent can make any new teacher anxious. Out of my binder, I pulled my parent questionnaire (last used in 2003) that I had sent out before conferences to get an idea of what was on parents' minds so I could prepare to meet their needs and requests. This was a timely and valuable resource to her. Through our conversation she had discovered within herself why she wanted it and how she would use it.

Pronoun Preferences

After reading an excerpt from Laura Lipton and Bruce Wellman's book *Mentoring Matters: A Practical Guide to Learning-Focused Relationships* (2003) on the different stances of coaching, collaborating, and consulting, I was interested to see how my pronoun use "Wordled out" in the conference transcript. As a consultant, I'd say *I*, as a collaborator I'd use *we*, and as a coach I'd use *you*.

With the "common words included" box checked, here's what Wordle showed me about the language of my questioning.

Overall, I stayed in my coaching stance using *you*, and I went into the consulting stance of *I* when I shared anecdotes that were related to that first-year teacher's questions and concerns.

As a busy educator, I don't take time to Wordle myself very often, but when I do, I take away new learning about myself as well as ideas about how to improve my teaching and coaching. Try it for yourself. What Wordles up for you?

Consider These Questions

Which words are repeated most in the classrooms in
    which you work?
What might Wordle out of your instruction?
What might Wordle out of the students' talk?
Which pronouns do you use in coaching?
After Wordling, what more do you know about yourself as a teacher
    and/or as a coach?

A Sponge Is
a Summary

Misconceptions are to understanding what crawling is to walking. We don't look at crawlers and say, "Too bad she's just crawling." We smile at the parents and say, "Pretty soon she'll be off and running." In the same way, misconceptions are a good sign that understanding is just around the corner. The more I teach, the more I can anticipate many misconceptions. Still, the unanticipated misconceptions constantly take me by surprise—and delight me.

I was in the car with my kindergartner on my husband's birthday when she asked, "What kind of restaurant are you taking him to tonight?"

"Italian," I said.

"Oh, I speak some Italian," she offered. *Wow,* I thought, *the things she learns in her class. How cool.*

"Would you teach me some words?"

"OK," she said. "I can count in Italian."

Ahna proceeded to draw straight lines in the air as she counted, "One, two, three, four" and then marked through them diagonally. "And five!" She grinned.

I looked in the rearview mirror questioningly. Italian? One, two, three, four, five?

She was a little cross with my confusion. "You know," she said. "In tally-an?"

"Tallies!" I blurted. "Oh, my goodness, *in tallies* sounds like *Italian*!"

Summarization is a strategy that is rife with misconceptions. Some, like Ahna's definition of "in tally-an," will catch us by surprise, but more are predictable. For a preassessment with intermediate students, I used a nonfiction passage about George Washington Carver's early life. The paragraph focused on two key ideas—that he loved plants and that going to school during that time was difficult for him.

Student Sample 1: The Wordy Summary

One student wrote as many sentences in a summary as existed in the original piece. "I didn't want to leave anything out," Clare told me when turning it in.

Misconception 1: Retell and summary are the same thing.

Most people agree: A summary should be shorter than the original text. As defined in the Free Online Dictionary it means *performed speedily and without ceremony.* Most students got this idea, but this was an easy misconception that we could clear up for those who didn't.

Student Sample 2: Repeat the First Sentence

Carver was born in Missouri around 1864.

Misconception 2: You can always find a topic sentence that summarizes the paragraph. It's usually first.

Most people agree: Many texts do not have an explicit topic sentence that captures the main idea of the passage. If such a sentence exists, it's usually not the first sentence. Richard Braddock from the University of Iowa studied contemporary writing in 1974 and found only 45% of topic sentences were traditional, simple topic sentences. I remember learning in school that the first sentence will tell you what a paragraph is going to be about. Although that was true for all the paragraphs we read designed for the task, in real life it would be true less than half of the time.

Student Sample 3: Topic Collector

George Washington Carver's life is what this is about.

Misconception 3: Topics and main ideas are the same thing.

Most people agree: Although the topic of the nonfiction passage was George Washington Carver's life, the main idea was that he loved plants and that it was difficult for him to go to school to study them. Summaries should be simple, but not so simple that the main idea is skipped.

Student Sample 4: Text-to-Self Connector

George Washington Carver was our first president. I didn't know it but he knew a lot about plants. I wouldn't have liked it if I couldn't go to school. He should've been able to do whatever he wanted.

Misconception 4: Schema is important and opinions matter.

Most people agree: In many aspects of literacy the text-to-self connection is important; however, everything you need to write a summary is already there in the text. There was certainly nothing about Carver being a president. Like a good therapist, there is no need for you to personally disclose while doing the job. A summary should include the main ideas of the text—not the ones you (as the summarizer) think you know, agree with, or like the best. Some students have trouble telling the difference between what is important to the author and what is important to the reader.

Taking Aim: Metaphors

When I'm working with a difficult concept, I like to hook kids' attention with a metaphor or an analogy. While doing the dishes, I thought about how a sponge holds water, but that when you squeeze it, you are left with the right amount of dampness to wipe down a counter. The point of a sponge is to be moist without being oversaturated. *Aha*, I thought: a sponge is a summary. We take hold of saturated text and squeeze out all the unnecessary details, keeping only what we need. Although there are limitations to this analogy, it's a start for kids who have little or no background knowledge with which to make their own connections.

Talking with the team of teachers concerned about students' lack of summarizing skills, I asked what students already knew about summaries.

"Not much," was the team's response. "Let's start from the beginning."

Here are some responses to the short-answer preassessment we gave to students, which asked, "What is a summary?"

"Something in the back of books."

"You are supposed to take all the words from the first sentence and rewrite it in your own words."

"Twenty words or less."

"Something you play with—or is it a sentence?"

"The time we are not in school." (*Summer . . . summery*)

"A ship." (*Summary . . .Submarine*)

It was clear that an engaging metaphor would be a good place to start. During my introductory lesson, I walked in with a bucket, sponge, chart, and marker. The students were curious. When they were gathered at my feet, I dipped the sponge into the bucket.

"This is a sponge," I said, and squeezed the water out. "I'm summarizing."

They reached to feel the damp sponge as I continued. "This is a summary. A sponge is a summary. Stay tuned. You'll be able to tell me why at the end of the lesson."

Rule-Based Summarization

Research from Marzano et al. (2004) tells us that effective summaries involve deleting, substituting, and keeping some information. To carry out these processes well, students must analyze the information they are working with in a complex way.

I told the students up front that we'd be using some rules to summarize. To help students visualize and remember the rules, we made up kinesthetic motions for them:

Keep (pull hands in to chest)
Delete (push hands away from body)
Substitute (cross hands to show movement)
Choose and write (mime pointing and writing)

Snapshot: Summarizing and Think-Aloud

Next, I did a think-aloud and modeled summarizing using a passage about the Amazon rainforest connecting to their theme study of the rainforest. Displaying the passage on chart paper, I read it aloud to the group. In my think-aloud, I noted that the author seemed to have a main idea about how the Amazon rainforest was getting smaller and how that was not a good thing. As I spoke, I circled four key words/ideas I chose to keep:

Amazon rainforest smaller deforestation Brazil

The rest of the passage I crossed out. "This is what I'm going to *delete*."

There was no need to *substitute* in that particular paragraph, but I gave them an example. "If the author wrote 'Birds, reptiles, and amphibians are affected by the loss of forest,' I could substitute the word *animals* and collapse the list of birds, reptiles, and amphibians."

Finally it was time to *choose* or *write*. We studied the first sentence and concluded that it did not capture the main idea. "Most paragraphs will not have the main idea stated in one sentence, and only sometimes is it the first one," I told them.

I wrote my summary sentence from the key words and ideas we kept:

In Brazil, the Amazon rainforest is shrinking because of deforestation, which is the loss of trees.

At that point I stopped and had them turn knee-to-knee with a partner and explain how I had applied the four rules of summarization in that paragraph. I smiled as they pointed at the chart, used the kinesthetic reminders of the rules, and explained how I'd summarized.

For the second paragraph, I asked them for help with what to keep and delete. When they suggested keeping small details, I had them look closely at what the author wanted us to keep that was most important. "Remember," I said, "we pull ourselves out of this. It's not what is most interesting or important to us. We are looking to summarize the author's words and what he or she is emphasizing."

A hand shot up. "Are you going to substitute where it says 'farmers, ranchers, and loggers'?"

"I am," I said, pleased with the application. We decided workers would suffice.

When it was time for the third paragraph, I handed out clipboards with the passage, and the students circled and crossed out words and phrases as we discussed them. On the blank lines below, we wrote our summary sentence. As the lesson drew to a close, we put our three summary sentences together and I said, "The summary should mostly be in the same order as the original text."

Sponge Metaphor

When I pulled my bucket back out, I repeated, "This is a sponge." I squeezed the water out and said, "I'm summarizing," and finally, "This is a summary. A sponge is a summary. Why?"

They turned back to their partners and discussed before we shared as a whole group.

"Well, the water you are squeezing out is like the words we are deleting from the paragraph."

"What else?" I probed.

"You kept some of the water in the sponge, just like we kept some of the words."

"What else?"

"You didn't add anything else to the summary sponge. It's just water. Like we aren't supposed to add other things we know or what we think is most interesting."

"What else?"

"The sponge and the summary both have a job to do."

The sponge lesson is just the beginning, the hook, to explicitly teach how to summarize by gradually releasing it to the students as they move toward independence. As the text becomes more difficult, so does the process of summarizing. Switching from nonfiction to fiction requires explicitly teaching a different summary approach.

"Wow, you readers and writers really soaked this up, didn't you?" They smiled and groaned.

Here is a review of the steps in this lesson:

1. Introduce the definition of *summary* by bringing in a bucket of water and a sponge. This analogy gives the children a visual image to hold in their minds as you practice summarizing together.
2. Tell the students you will be using some rules to summarize. List the rules. To help students visualize and remember the rules, make up kinesthetic motions for them—or use mine.
3. Do a think-aloud and model summarizing by using a short passage that is low level and high interest for starters.
4. Return to your bucket and sponge. Review what the students have learned by asking them what is important to know about a summary.

Consider These Questions

What is your view of the importance of misconceptions?

Which description of misconceptions is true for the students with whom you work?

Have you taught rule-based summarization before?

What do you think about having students start by physically deleting text from a copied passage? How long might you keep them at that stage before transitioning them to doing it in their head?

How is this different from a strategy that challenges students to limit summaries to ten words or some set amount? How is it the same?

Wii Summary

"The summaries my sixth graders write are just awful," Ingrid said when we met.

"How much time would you estimate that you've spent teaching them explicit summarization strategies?" I asked.

Pause.

"Sixth graders should know how to summarize by now," she said.

That would be nice, wouldn't it? Oh, how I empathized with those sixth graders as I recently faced a difficult summarizing task myself. At a Friday coaches' meeting, I was to give a "state of the state" summary of what is happening regarding a national initiative in the areas of teacher evaluation and standards. I found myself sifting through the notes of three different meetings as I tried to keep the important ideas, delete the smaller details, substitute some words (i.e., *subjects* instead of listing *math, reading, writing*), and put it in my own words. The more I immersed myself in summarization, the more I understood what makes it difficult for students and teachers alike.

Emily Kissner's book *Summarizing, Paraphrasing, and Retelling: Skills for Better Reading, Writing, and Test Taking* deepened my knowledge of all that goes into summarization, and one of my favorite quotes from her book came to mind when Ingrid told me, "Sixth graders should know how to summarize by now."

> *Saying that students should have "learned" these skills in a previous class or grade is like saying that students should have learned how to write in first grade and therefore need no more instruction in the topic. The logic just doesn't work. (Kissner 2006, 4)*

When I replied to Ingrid, I wasn't worried about the awfulness of the student summaries or what they had been taught about them in the past. All we can do is move forward. "Let's look at the summaries to plan our work," I said.

Not Just I-Do, Not Just You-Do, But We-Do Too

On my Wii Fit for the bodywork in yoga and strength training, I chose a male trainer, whom I named Lii. Attempting the downward-dog pose, for example, Lii offered me a demo. "Before we start, I'll show you how it's done." He gave me all sorts of tips, such as, "Make sure your elbows are facing outward" and "Keep your eyes on your stomach." Then he asked me, "Are you ready to try it yourself? Let's do it together." During my thirty-second pose, Lii monitored my progress based on how I was pressing on the Wii board and said, "You are putting too much weight on your feet." When I adjusted, he said, "Great—that's it." At the end I got a quick assessment. That time I got only two out of four stars, but he assured me that I would do better when I put more weight on my hands.

What I find, and what I discovered was true in Ingrid's classroom, is that some complex skills such as summarization are taught in only two modes: all teacher (I-do) or all students (you-do). In the I-do mode, teachers can easily be led to think that the kids get it, because the smart ones offer to answer our questions, and everyone else nods to make us happy when we ask, "Does that make sense?"

In the you-do mode, that illusion falls apart with a chorus of "I don't get it" or when we receive work that misses the mark. That's where the students were when Ingrid deemed their progress "awful." In between those two modes is an entire continuum of we-do (or Wii-do) that has many of the components of my living-room interactive game.

Planning Gradual Release

Ingrid and I both agreed that the goal was having her sixth graders independently summarize a variety of texts. To start our work, we read an excerpt from *Summarizing, Paraphrasing, and Retelling*. In it, Kissner talks about the "rules of summarization" and reminds us, "We all know just telling children what the rules are doesn't mean that they know how to apply them" (18).

With my Wii trainer Lii in mind, we planned how we could *demonstrate* to students what rule-based summarization might look like. These are the "rules" we would use:

1. *Keep.*
2. *Delete.*
3. *Substitute.*
4. *Choose a topic sentence or rewrite.*

Sitting at Ingrid's table, I reached for an excerpt from *Frogs* by Nic Bishop (2008). I showed Ingrid how I would model circling the key words such as *frogs, escape, jump, hide,* and *predators.* Then I would cross out all the other words. Using a think-aloud, I would construct my summary sentence with the key ideas and come up with something like, "Many frogs escape from predators by jumping and hiding." Ingrid liked the idea of physically annotating the text to make the "keep" and "delete" tasks very concrete.

"This is harder than I thought," she mused.

"After my demonstration," I said, "I would release responsibility just a little bit to the students. Moving on to the next paragraph, I would read it aloud and then have students suggest what I could keep and delete in shared writing. I'd hand over my pen and let one student delete and another student scribe as we create our summary statement."

Ingrid noted there were several specific facts about African bullfrogs and poison dart frogs used as support. "My students won't know which of those details to include," she said.

"You're right, which is why we are still guiding. If we look at all the details the author chose, we can see how he's using them for support, but the important or main idea is that frogs have unique ways to avoid predators."

As we worked our way through the excerpt, we talked about which student misconceptions might arise, what they might be able to do with the help of others, and what would be necessary to explicitly teach and have them practice.

I added, "Remember this is all straightforward nonfiction that is below grade level to give students practice and confidence before we increase the difficulty."

Scaffolding Toward Independence

Here is the teaching sequence that Ingrid and I developed:

Day 1: Teacher models; students listen, notice, and question.

Day 2: Teacher begins to model; students listen, suggest key words, and delete text; and one or more students scribe the shared summary statement.

Day 3: Teacher selects a section to summarize together, and students circle key words, delete text, and write shared summary statement on their own copy of the same passage.

Day 4: Teacher strategically partners students. Pairs summarize by circling key words, deleting text, substituting if necessary, and writing a summary statement. Students are in proximity to each other and teacher for support.

Day 5: Students try a paragraph on their own and then check with their partner for support.

Day 6: Students summarize independently while teacher pulls a small group for strategic support.

As with every plan, our actual practice differed. For example Day 4 became Days 4, 5, and 6, because the partnering was very well received and an effective way to balance some "give-it-a-go" time with "support." We ended up working through the gradual release of responsibility for summarization of nonfiction text over about ten days.

Change Happens

On Day 8 I was at a conference when I received this email:

> Heather,
> Based on our work today there are eighteen kids that are writing some pretty good summaries, but I had nine at my small group. That seems like too many. I'm going to extend the work tomorrow and run two different small groups or maybe even three.
>
> What surprises me is that we've really only summarized two or three different articles. In the past, I would have had my students summarizing at least one article a day, but they are really understanding the process so it's easier to let that go. And they like it. It seems like by offering more guidance, they are having fun with it.
>
> I know you said that summarization looks different for different types of text and needs to be taught that way. We'll be starting a unit next month on historical fiction, and I wondered if we could do something similar with how to summarize narrative text?
> Ingrid

Because of Ingrid's openness and willingness to learn and change, she went from "Students write awful summaries and should know how to do it" to "Students understand and have fun when we take it slow and I guide them." As Lii would say, "Well done."

Consider These Questions

Do you often summarize pieces before asking students to summarize? What do you notice about your thinking?

How much time would you estimate that you've spent teaching explicit summarization strategies?

Between the teacher modeling and the students working independently, there is a whole continuum of instruction that needs to take place. How do you flexibly plan for a gradual release of responsibility?

Summarization is much more than a test-taking skill. What increases relevance for learners in writing summaries?

Presenting Knowledge

I hear and I forget; I see and I remember; I do and I understand.

—Chinese Proverb

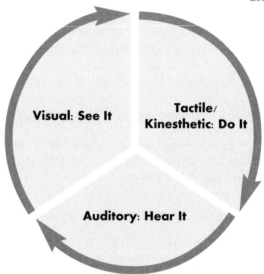

Whereas my son would check the box in any survey for "likes to learn by reading or being told about new content," my husband would not. He's an architectural designer and a builder, so he learns visually and by doing things with his hands. My middle daughter, an artist, also needs visual cueing; learning through the auditory mode is very difficult for her. Ahna, my youngest, is a mover and shaker and learns things by touching, moving, and experiencing.

It turns out my family is a lot like our population. Whether we call it intelligences, learning styles, or modalities, we know that people learn differently, and when their learning needs are met, they learn best.

Many classrooms share content predominantly by telling about it or reading about it.

As educators we know our classrooms include tactile/kinesthetic and visual learners. Embracing nonlinguistic (not reading or talking) represen-

86

tation is an important consideration for teaching and learning today. Research as well as experience points us to the conclusion that the more we use both systems—linguistic and the nonlinguistic—the better we can think about and use knowledge.

Inputs and Outputs

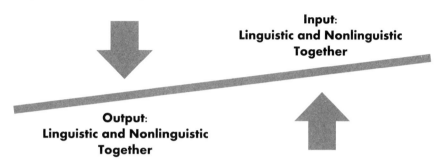

There are two ways to think about nonlinguistic representation: as inputs and outputs. On the input side of things, we teachers are responsible for making sure we share information in multiple ways. For example, we can introduce new content about the Bill of Rights by giving ten pictures to students and saying, "These are ten rights we enjoy as citizens. Look at the pictures and predict the rights they represent." Our brains love pictures and puzzles. As our eyes are studying a picture of protesters, our brains are trying to make as many associations as possible. Freedom of speech may come to mind or not. Either way this anticipation has us engaged in a way that opening up the textbook to page 75 and reading about the Bill of Rights may not. Taking the next step and combining the pictures with the text of the rights helps us use the linguistic and nonlinguistic systems together. In this scenario, the input of new knowledge was designed by the teacher in two ways that could create new pathways of thought in students' brains.

Output is what we do with new knowledge. We could talk about it, write about it, draw, act, sing, and more. What is most commonly requested of students in the classroom is the linguistic: write or tell. As with the input stage, using both systems helps students use and remember the knowledge. When it comes time to check in with students about how they are making sense of the Bill of Rights, we could ask them to act out the rights. A student who stands in front of a door, shakes his head, and holds his hand up as if to stop someone could be representing Amendment III and showing an understanding of the need for an owner's consent to quarter troops. Kids who express themselves physically would connect with this activity.

Two issues make output complex. The first is how to use nonlinguistic representation to elaborate on knowledge. The second is that nonlinguistic representation needs to be scaffolded, not just assigned.

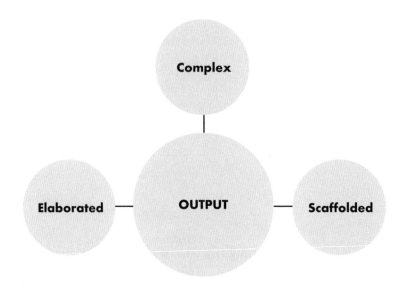

In our Bill of Rights scenario, students were investigating a knowledge-level question: what is the Bill of Rights? This foundational information builds toward other levels of questioning and can move students to consider, Why are these rights important to me and to all citizens in a democratic society? To respond to that question, they would need to elaborate on their knowledge. This is why we teach civics.

We might ask students to choose an amendment that preserves an important personal right and write a rap about it. A rap? I'm all over that. I love music, rhythm, and expression. I would rush home, find a beat, and lay out some lyrics. But that's not true for all learners. For many, participating in this nonlinguistic representation requires some scaffolding.

Let's take Teachers A and B, who noticed that their fifth graders love and respond to music and decided that for a culminating project, the students would write Amendment Raps. Teacher A gave the students the list of amendments and criteria for how the raps would be scored. She said there would be some in-class time and some homework. Raps were due in three days. Three days later, the students performed their raps. Some were works of art, like Mario's and Chen's. Most were at the surface level along the lines of, "Freedom of speech gives me to the right to stand up here and rap, all right?" Several were thrown together at the last minute. She was disappointed that not all the kids' projects rose to the level of Mario's and Chen's.

Teacher B also gave students a list of amendments and criteria for scoring, and then she shared a model, "Right to trial by jury," with them. She said, "Writing a rap might seem easy at first, but it's actually quite difficult. There are several parts you need to consider." They watched a YouTube on how to be a rapper, and she gave them three websites to look at that give tips on creating raps. Their assignment that night was to pick an amendment and write a paragraph on why that particular right spoke to them. She read the paragraphs and offered brief refocusing feedback to five students. Then the students took the paragraphs and circled key words that might be used in their rap. At that point Teacher B pulled out rhyming dictionaries that she'd borrowed from the library. For the next assignment students were asked to collect their backup music or a rap they wanted to mimic written on an index card. When six students "couldn't find anything," she gave them a rap track on a CD to use. Because she knew her population of kids, she knew not all of them would have the resources to be able to complete the task. She encouraged them to try to write two or three stanzas and to stay focused on why the amendment right was so important. She used her model "Right to trial by jury" to show them how she made connections between what fairness means to her and the amendment. Three days after the start of the project, they were ready to perform. She was impressed with the quality of student work.

Teacher A assigned; Teacher B scaffolded the task by providing a model and breaking it down into sub-skills she knew the students would need. To have students using nonlinguistic representation effectively in the output mode, they need scaffolding.

A teacher who is assigning . . .
- may not have ever tried the task him/herself,
- provides a menu or description of the task,
- explains scoring criteria,
- clearly defines a timeline of when the project is due, and
- offers time for completion.

A teacher who is scaffolding . . .
- previews the task and understands what is difficult about it and which skills may be required,
- in addition to a menu or description, shares the qualities or traits of what makes a good product,
- shares a personal or past student model and connects it to the scoring criteria,
- breaks the timeline up into shorter tasks and gives feedback as well as needed support to individuals along the way, and
- offers time for completion as well as explicitly defined tasks for those students who need it.

Putting It All Together

When I'm planning for a lesson or unit with teachers, I think, How would I need to learn this? How about my husband? My son? My daughters? Separating the input (how I present new information) from the output (how students represent understanding) helps me keep my learners in mind. Further, considering how students can elaborate on knowledge and how I'm scaffolding versus assigning helps me create tasks for learners to complete that allow them to express their individual gifts as well as stretch themselves.

Reflecting on the opening proverb—I hear and I forget; I see and I remember; I do and I understand—I'm working to move past the forgetting and remembering to a place of understanding. It's a challenge, and it's worth it.

Consider These Questions

What came to mind when you read the opening proverb?

What is your predominant style? How about your colleagues and family members?

How do you plan to connect the linguistic with the nonlinguistic? Do some subjects or topics lend themselves more easily to this?

How do you use nonlinguistic representation to have students elaborate on their knowledge?

What is the difference, for you, between scaffolding and assigning?

Two-Thirds Boys, One-Third Girls: Coaching Nonlinguistic Representation

Hannah was in her second year of teaching when we began our work together. She was interested in "bettering her game," as she put it. "I know I have lots that I could work on, but I'm not sure where to start," she admitted in our initial meeting.

"That's fine," I said. "Determining your focus often comes after we get started. Tell me what you love about teaching."

"This is what I wanted to do since I was a little girl," she said. "I work with some challenging kids, and I want to have high expectations for every one of them. I also love how they come together as a community—well, sometimes."

I made notes and asked her what gets in the way sometimes.

"I have a really active class this year. Two-thirds boys and one-third girls, so I worry sometimes that the boys are overpowering the girls just by sheer numbers. Sometimes cooperative learning activities get out of control or kids don't seem to know what they are supposed to be doing. Like I said, I know I have lots I can work on."

After our meeting, I stayed and transcribed the first part of a math lesson. In my transcripts it was clear that there were some significant differences between the boys and girls in both the behaviors and the level of comprehension. On my way out, I emailed the transcript to Hannah and told her we could discuss it the next day when we met. I take the "hot potato" approach with transcripts and try to hand them over to the teacher as soon as possible. Because some principals do transcripts of teaching, I want to differentiate mine from evaluation. I am not the keeper of the transcript, only the recorder. Some teachers read them right away, and others hang on to them until we have a chance to talk.

Noticing Patterns

I wheeled my cart of coaching materials in as Hannah led her class to a specialist. I keep a class set of pencils, index cards, a couple of professional books, markers, my binder, and chart paper in my cart; I'm never exactly sure what I might need.

"The boy-girl thing was really noticeable in the transcript," she said as she returned.

"In what way?" I asked.

"The boys were constantly asking me to repeat directions and would say things like, 'What are we doing?' I praised the girls and used them as examples for role models. It got me to wondering if I'm not giving directions in a way that's clear for the boys. It seemed like several were confused."

I smiled. Some teachers with the same information as Hannah would talk about how rowdy the boys were or how they never paid attention, but Hannah turned it around to look at what she might do as a teacher. Perhaps changing her behavior would have an effect on their behavior. "You mentioned before that the boys seemed to be very active learners and visual too," I commented. "How often do you incorporate visual or kinesthetic cues into your directions?"

"I don't even know what that would be like," Hannah admitted. "I'm not sure I've seen that done before."

We planned a lesson for the next period in math. After she led the opening daily math review, I would introduce the activity. The kids were working on line math puzzles, which required them to arrange a set of digits so the sums were the same on the vertical, the horizontal, and the diagonal (in the more challenging puzzles). The students would be working in partners, and there were multistep directions. It was an ideal opportunity to model.

"What do you want to watch for when I'm teaching?" I asked Hannah.

"I want to see how the boys respond differently," she said.

"How will you know if they are responding differently?" I asked.

"I suppose they'll say, 'What are we doing?' less often," she replied.

I nodded. That seemed like a logical, informal way to start measuring what we were trying.

Chart Paper, Fingers, and Repeat

As Hannah wrapped up the daily math review, she told the students they'd be working with their math partners.

"Could I write those on chart paper as you are saying them so there is a place to look if we forget?" I asked, pulling out my chart paper.

She nodded. I stood next to her, recorded the partner names, and stuck the chart paper up front. With two kids absent, we need to reconfigure partners in two groups, but everyone was clear about who was working with whom.

When I took the lead, Hannah moved to the side with her notebook. I began by modeling a simple line math puzzle on the board. By drawing quick sketches of the materials they'd be using, I showed the paper cup with the digit on paper squares inside, the templates for the puzzle, and a pencil. Then I wrote 1, 2, and 3 on the whiteboard and listed the steps.

"Everyone hold up one finger," I requested. The students held up their pointer fingers.

"The first thing you will do is find a space with your partner, and the taller partner will go get the supplies." I wrote on the whiteboard:

1. Taller gets supplies.

"Now show me two fingers," I said. The students made the peace sign.

"The second thing you will do is try to place the digits so you get the same sum going vertically and horizontally. When I say *sum*, I want you to put your hands in balance so you remember that they need to be equal. When I say *vertical*, I want you to raise one arm like this, and when I say *horizontal*, I want you to slice your arm like that."

2. Place digits so vertical and horizontal sum is the same.

"Hold up three fingers. The third and last thing you will do is take the pencil and write the digits in the correct boxes after you have checked that the sums are the same."

3. Check. Move digits and write in pencil. Go on to next puzzle.

"I'm going to count to ten slowly, and I'd like you to move on the carpet so you are sitting next to your math partner. I've seen how well you cooperate, so I know you can do this. One . . . two . . . three . . ." The kids moved around so they were sitting next to their partners.

"Well done. Now, the person sitting closer to me is going to tell what we are going to do first. Then the other partner will tell what we are going to do second. And then the first partner will finish up and tell what we are going to do third. You can use the steps on the board to help you. Turn knee-to-knee, eye-to-eye with your partner." I waited. "Begin."

Most partners were retelling the directions in an animated way, but two different partner pairs were struggling, so I moved to assist them. Within a minute I gave the "quiet" signal to everyone and asked what questions they had.

"What if we don't agree with the other's answer?" a student asked.

"What will you do if you don't agree? That's a good question," I said.

"We could work it again and check it," said the same student.

After questions, the students went to work. Upon finding spots to work, the taller students gathered the paper cups, templates, and pencils. Then the kids pulled out the digits and started placing them on the squares and finding sums. Hannah and I moved around, observing groups. I was pleased that the first two puzzles were less difficult so that students were able to practice the structure before the math got more difficult. They spent almost twenty minutes solving puzzles as we made anecdotal notes about what we were observing.

Recess Debrief

We had less than ten minutes to debrief the lesson, but Hannah said, "OK, so you used the chart paper to record the partners, which is simple. But it's not something I've taken the time to do, so kids always have to ask me when they forget. Then you drew the supplies so they knew what to gather. I love that. Just little sketches, but everyone had what they needed, and then you rehearsed the directions by having them move and look at the chart. There was only one kid who didn't know what to do, but all I had to do was point to the board and then he was back on track. Then you had them repeat the directions, which I thought was going to take too long, but I really think that spending the time up front meant they could do the work, because they knew what to do."

"I think about giving kids tools around the room through pictures or movements to help them remember multistep directions," I said. "I certainly wouldn't go to this level of detail with all lessons, but this one required some extra management with materials and partners. Some kids just don't get it through auditory alone."

"The funny thing is," admitted Hannah, "I don't either. I'm a very visual person. I've just never connected that to directions."

What I didn't know was that Hannah was a gifted cartoonist. Once she got the idea for drawing sketches of supplies or steps in a process, she was hooked. I've peeked in her room over the years, and her charts and boards clearly direct what is happening. Students use the linguistic and nonlinguistic reminders to keep them on track.

Consider These Questions

In this coaching cycle, Hannah noticed her boy-girl patterns, but if she hadn't, in what ways might the transcript have supported a professional conversation about gender differences and comprehension in the classroom?

How do you use nonlinguistic representation while giving directions?

There is a balance between under- and overstructuring activities in the direction phase. How do you achieve balance?

What strategies do you use to keep your coaching debriefs short and focused?

Getting and Giving Student Feedback

I saved this quote from an email with the title "Why We Love Children" (http://officespam.chattablogs.com/archives/2006/10/why-we-love-children.html):

> "A little girl had just finished her first week of school. 'I'm just wasting my time,' she said to her mother. 'I can't read, I can't write, and they won't let me talk!'"

I'll be the first to admit I enjoy the sound of my own voice. I love to tell stories. I love it when people laugh at just the right part or when I scan the room and all eyes are on me as my listeners wait for the next line. But I also enjoy a good Malbec wine, and I know too much of that isn't good for me either.

I learned to pipe down in my personal life about eight years ago when my middle daughter, Maya, began to stutter. When she was unable to get through a short sentence without bursting into tears, we visited a speech specialist. My homework assignment was to record our dinnertime conversation. If a normal conversation had a typical number of verbal demands, in our family it was four times the expected amount. My husband and I talk a lot, and Maya's older brother is constantly talking. Although her vocabulary development was three years ahead of her chronological age, she still had the brain of the three-year-old who was unable to keep up with the verbal demands. As I took this in, I paraphrased the speech specialist, saying, "Basically the issue isn't Maya's brain or speech—it's us that need some shut-up therapy." The specialist was sweet; she just smiled and said nothing.

Recent research finds that feedback is most effective when teachers understand how students are making sense of their learning experiences. John Hattie writes about this in his book *Visible Learning*:

> *The mistake I was making was seeing feedback as something teachers provided to students. . . . It was only when I discovered that feedback was most powerful when it is from the student to the teacher that I started to understand it better. When teachers seek, or at least are open to, feedback from students as to what*

*students know, what they understand, where they make errors, when they
have misconceptions, when they are not engaged—then teaching and learning
can be synchronized and powerful. Feedback to teachers helps make learning
visible. (Hattie 2009, 73).*

When I consider who the best-educated and most experienced thinker
in the classroom is, the answer is almost always the teacher. If I am understanding how the students are making meaning, I can adapt the questions,
lessons, and interventions. The only way for me to have access to that information is to get it in the form of kid talk—lots of it, and in writing too.
Schema, 10:2 theory, and exit slips are ways to seek feedback about students' understanding.

Schema: Theirs, Not Mine

A friend of mine, Nari, is a student support manager and was working
with the kindergartners on the playground.

"Please don't run on the concrete" she said.

"OK!" said a five-year-old as she was running off.

"Please don't run on the concrete," Nari said again.

"OK!" said another kindergartner. "Wait—what is *concrete*?"

We laughed because those sweet kids were more than willing not to
run on concrete; they just didn't know what it was. Because we aren't five
or seven or even fifteen years old anymore, we can't know what's in kids'
heads or how they are comprehending the information they are taking in.

Two ways to quickly assess schema are the quick-sketch and the quick-
write methods. Because I'm not ten in this day and age, I know I have different schema for the word *clustering* that I'm going to teach as a prewriting
technique to fourth graders. When I think of clustering, clusters of grapes
come to mind, but I ask students to draw a quick sketch on a piece of paper
for thirty seconds of what comes up when I say *cluster*. They think of choco-
late-peanut clusters, video game clusters, bomb clusters, and more. Some
have no associations at all. I take a moment to connect grapes to peanut
clusters to video games and bomb clusters and point out that all of those
examples have similar elements bunched together and that's what we are
going to do in writing. That's how I connect to their experience and support meaning making.

10:2 Theory

Ten and two (10:2) theory is based on the idea that students make sense of
new information by periodically integrating it with existing information.
As learners, we naturally take mental breaks to absorb information even
as more information is presented. Mary Budd Rowe (*Journal of Teacher Education*, 1986) explains how teachers can provide regular pauses to accom-
modate this need. She recommends we pause for two minutes about every
ten minutes (thus the 10:2 theory).

Understanding this idea in theory and actually putting it into practice are two different things. Talking faster to cram more in the ten-minute window or simply directing, "Now turn and talk to integrate what you've learned into your existing thinking" are not highly effective. I think about the ebb and flow of feedback in the teaching and learning cycles. During flow, I am modeling, thinking aloud, demonstrating, and actively practicing. Then as my teaching ebbs, I'm providing students with the opportunity for talk, writing, and feedback. I use a timer to raise my awareness of the pacing and chunk my instruction to let kids make meaning.

Exit Slips

These are also known as "Did they get it?" receipts, and I use them often. My favorite question to ask is, "What was the most important thing you learned in _____ (subject) today?" Here was a response that I received after a revision lesson: "I learned that revision is checking your spelling." Another good one: "I learned that elaboration is writing many words in a sentence." Even better: "I learned that a summary is copying down what was already written."

My response each time was to clap my hand on my forehead and moan, but when I was finished doing that, I was thankful for the informal assessment of student understanding. The clearer I am about students' thinking and misconceptions, the less likely I am to fall under the illusion that everyone is getting it. I use exit slips as five-minute quick-writes that can be preceded by talk to help students reflect on their learning and critical thinking. Most often I use them at the end of the lesson, but they can also be used as we transition during the lesson.

Here are a few other questions/prompts I've used:

- *I understand . . . but I do not understand . . .*
- *One question I have is . . .*
- *Three words/phrases I heard a lot during this lesson were . . .*
- *I know _____ is true because . . .*
- *I smiled/frowned today when . . .*

For students who are not writing words or sentences yet I've used these:

- *Draw a picture of yourself learning today.*
- *Draw a picture of what your face looked like when you learned _____.*
- *I could/could not (circle one) tell a friend about what I learned.*
- *Draw the most important thing about _____.*

Although it may sound like a Geico commercial, five minutes spent on feedback before, during, and at the end of the lesson can save . . . a lot. After a lesson that doesn't quite work, I always ask myself these questions:

How did I connect to the students' schema?
Did I give them multiple opportunities to talk, write, and think?
What did they take away from the learning experience?
How do I know?

There's Been a Misblunderstanding About Feedback

If you aren't already familiar with Becky Botsford (aka WordGirl) and her sidekick Captain Huggy Face on PBS's WordGirl (http://pbskids.org/word-girl), you should check out her powers. Even if you don't think it's a cool way to pique kids' interest in vocabulary, there are humorous and important lessons for us all.

In one episode, WordGirl tries to prevent the Butcher (one of the mere mortal villains prone to pastrami attacks) from robbing a grocery store. While he's trying to rob the store, the manager keeps offering him a job selling the grocer's meat. WordGirl comes to the rescue:

WordGirl: It seems there is a bit of a misunderstanding here.
Butcher: Yes, I said it was a misblunderstanding.
WordGirl: *Misblunderstanding* is not a word. A misunderstanding is
 when you have the wrong idea about something.

Of course she saves the grocery store and takes care of the butcher. Along the way WordGirl got me thinking about misblunderstandings in education.

I'm in a fourth-grade classroom and it's November. At the beginning of a coaching cycle, the teacher says she has reluctant writers and wants to know what she can do about it. She feels like she's working way too hard.

There are forty minutes on the schedule for writing, and I transcribe on my laptop the whole time. I type until my fingers are sore. There are big monologue blocks: all her. The teacher is intelligent and models great ideas in her writing. Every once in awhile she throws out a question for a few kids to answer sequentially in teacher-student volleyball. During the last eight minutes of the lesson, she passes out paper and tells her students to "get started." A couple of them stare at her and look up at all she's written on the board. When the bell rings for recess, the kids hurriedly pass in writing.

During our debrief we begin by looking at the student work.

"See?" she says. "They aren't putting out any effort."

I ask, "How much do you want to be talking and modeling in relation to the kids writing and talking about their writing?"

"I wanted them to have at least a paragraph. I guess it just all took too long to get going."

Then she notes thirty-two minutes of talking and eight minutes of writing from the transcript.

She laughs. "I'm thinking of one of those hourglasses. I'd like it to be the exact opposite: thirty-two minutes of writing and eight of talking."

I say, "It's true that writers get better by writing. Would that be a good focus for our work?"

With her openness, I suggest we look at the lesson and pick places where the students could do the talking and the writing instead of the teacher. Together we rewrite the lesson plan, and she asks me to teach it the next day. I stop to think, What's the purpose of me modeling? Sometimes teachers ask me to model when they feel unsure about teaching something, but observing my model can actually make them feel less confident in themselves. That's not my goal, so I ask her what the purpose is of having me teach. She clearly wants to see what is possible.

"I want to watch my reluctant writers from a new perspective. Maybe I won't be so frustrated with them if I'm observing."

Demonstrating

It's 10:31 am and we're sitting together at the group meeting space.

Coach: Good morning, everyone. Today we are going to work on elaboration in our writing. [*Writes* elaboration *on the board.*] I'm going to count to ten and have you turn knee-to-knee and eye-to-eye with a partner. Go. [*Counts down.*] Thank you. The partner closer to me will go first; please raise your hand if you are the partner closer to me. Thank you. [*Helps one unsure partner.*] You are going to go back and forth with that partner with what you already know about elaboration. [*Models with one student.*] You'll have one minute. Go. [*Writes down what students are saying and gives quiet signal when one-minute timer sounds.*]

[*10:33*] **Coach:** Please thank your partner. Someone said *elaboration* has the word *lab* in it. Someone said it is like the word *expand* in writing. Many of you talked about how it is telling more. To elaborate in writing is to use details to make writing very clear for our readers. That's what we are going to do today. Now read this paragraph silently to yourself [*puts up chart paper with paragraph with little to no elaboration*] and think, Does this have elaboration? [*Gives reading time.*] May I have a brave and courageous reader read this aloud? [*Student reads.*] Turn back to your partner knee-to-knee and eye-to-eye. The other partner will go first. Tell your partner whether you think this has elaboration or not. Each of you will have thirty seconds. What are your questions?

Student: What if we don't agree?

Coach: That's OK right now. I just want you to talk about what you see as elaboration in writing.

[10:37] **Coach:** Please thank your partner. I heard many of you say that there isn't much elaboration in this paragraph—there aren't a lot of details that make it clear. At your seats you left your journals open to a blank page. When you get there, please write the word *elaboration* at the top. I'm going to give you two minutes of freewriting to write everything you know about elaboration so far. You'll have a chance to do this again at the end of the class as well. Let's start writing in our journals.

[10:40] [*All students are freewriting on elaboration while coach checks on individuals.*]

The lesson goes on from here. The students share their writing with a partner and then write a couple of sentences of a nonexample for elaboration based on a choice of topics. It surprises me how much students like to produce "writing that needs help." Then they take the nonexample and rewrite it with elements of elaboration. These are read aloud, and their partners point out where they hear elaboration. We talk about how each of the ideas is really tightly connected.

At the end of the class, students take another two minutes to write about what they know about elaboration so far. During the debrief, the teacher and I look at the students' journals together.

The teacher shares, "Some of these kids covered the front and back of the page. I haven't seen them write like this before. They were talking with each other. No offense, but you didn't seem to be working as hard as I usually am, running around putting out fires and trying to get kids to write. How can I get them to do this when you aren't here?"

Our instructional coaching model is based on gradual release, with the goal of doing exactly what the teacher requested—"doing the same things successfully without me [the coach] there." Because the goal was to increase writing and decrease teacher talk, we began by planning mini-lessons intentionally. Limiting talk to less than ten minutes before we had the kids either writing or talking about writing was the objective. Some days I taught, and some days she taught. We watched the kids respond with enthusiasm, and their ability to sustain writing grew longer and longer. When we hit obstacles with writers, we studied them together. A few weeks later, I came back to do another transcript when the teacher felt she was ready. On my way out of the classroom I left a note on her computer: "You flipped the hourglass."

Learning from Misblunderstandings

I believe there are two misblunderstandings at play here and in many of our classrooms. There is a myth that teacher talking is the same thing as teaching. We need to switch our focus from what the teacher is saying and doing to what the students are saying and doing. Just because she said it doesn't mean she taught it. If kids aren't doing something independently (like fourth graders generating a paragraph), we can begin where they are. What can they do independently? Make a list? Write a couple of sentences? Start there. Give them guided and independent time to write, and time to talk about their writing as real writers. Those aren't luxuries to enjoy if we have time—this is teaching writing.

While coaching, I could've chosen to work on the symptoms by zeroing in on a list of reluctant writers, but I believe that would've been another misunderstanding. The reluctant writers weren't the source of the challenge. In my role as a "kidwatcher," I saw students whispering and giggling after ten minutes of passive time. The teacher worked hard—really hard—to keep their attention for thirty minutes, and then asked them to write. To me, that would've been like my golf coach filling my head with tips for a half hour and then handing me a bag and saying, "Go to it, Rader." I would've been a reluctant golfer too!

From experience, I've learned that when a teacher says, "I feel like I'm working too hard," it probably means the kids haven't learned yet how to work hard themselves. The students in this situation benefited from guided practice, and so did the teacher.

Why do I recognize too much teacher talk? Because it's been true for me too. And when did I talk too much? When I didn't know how to skillfully and gradually release the practice and independence to students. What would I have wanted in that situation? Someone to gently guide me to a different way that felt more efficient for me and more effective for my students. Every child deserves the opportunity to practice real, careful, and critical writing . . . and every teacher deserves to provide those experiences.

Consider These Questions

What misblunderstandings arise in your setting? What is the effect?
For which purposes do you decide to model or demonstrate?
How prevalent is "too much teacher talk" in the classroom?
What do you anticipate might've been some of the steps to gradually
    release the teaching from coach to teacher?

Explicitly Teaching Writing

Overprompting of Young Writers

I have been teaching long enough to remember a time before our large-scale state writing assessment when the word *prompt* wasn't connected to writing. Yet after receiving our first set of unfortunate writing scores years ago, my team bought a book of more than one hundred "everyday" prompts. Our well-intentioned assumption was that if teaching kids to respond to a prompt helped, then having them respond to prompts frequently would really increase their success. Some teachers tell me their students respond to a writing prompt every day. Here are a few prompts to which I've read student responses:

> *Write about your favorite TV program.*
> *Write about a time you wished you could fly.*
> *You discover a magic egg. Tell the story of what happens next.*

Although many kids will dutifully write to these starters, their responses are often formulaic, lacking both elaboration and voice. For every prompt, there are children who struggle with it. Maybe seven. Maybe three. Or if you are lucky, just one, and his name might be Zachary. When Zachary tries on the prompt, it doesn't fit.

What the prompt says: *Write about your favorite TV program.*

What Zachary says: "I don't watch TV."

What the prompt says: *Write about a time you wished you could fly.*

What Zachary says: "I'm afraid of heights."

What the prompt says: *You discover a magic egg. Tell the story of what happens next.*

What Zachary says: "I think magic eggs are stupid."

The obstacle is that one prompt doesn't fit all, because kids need to make personal connections to their writing topics.

Students Need to Make Prompts Their Own

Before we go swishing the prompts out with the bathwater, let me say there is a place for them. Beyond large-scale assessments, students need to write to a prompt when they are filling out college forms and scholarship applications, or applying for a job. Vicki Spandel reminds us in her book *Creating Writers Through 6-Trait Writing Assessment and Instruction* (2005) that there are a few decent prompts that provide multiple entry points for writers. In addition, it's our treatment of a prompt that can make or break it.

Students can make a personal connection to prompts in these ways:

- Reading or listening to related high-quality mentor texts
- Talking with their classmates about unique approaches to the writing
- Brainstorming lists as a whole group and individually
- Challenging the prompt with a turnaround

Let me say a little more about "challenging the prompt." If Zachary is prompted to "Describe a delicious meal" but what he really wants to write about is the disgusting pea soup and crusty dry bread that Grandma made on Sunday, I want the bread-and-soup writing. When young writers balk at a prompt, ask them, "Is the opposite more true for you?" and "By changing a word or two, can we make it fit better?"

Prompts Are the Beginning, Not the Finish Line

If the purpose of a prompt is to get students writing, then we shouldn't expect it to also be the finish line. This came to light when students in our district, kindergarten through sixth grade, wrote in January about a time they were hurt. Some teachers were confused with what the selection committee made up of teachers and instructional coaches found to be proficient writing. For example, one child began by writing about the time he got hurt, his grandma gave him a Band-Aid, and her dog, Sadie, came up to lick him. Most of the paper was about his obvious affection for Sadie.

A colleague challenged this paper, saying, "It's more about the dog than it is about the hurt. Why isn't this off prompt?"

I asked, "Did the child write?"

"Yes."

"And can you tell he read the prompt?"

"Yes, but only because he mentioned the Band-Aid."

"Then the prompt did its job, because the child wrote a high-quality piece that began with an idea *prompted* by 'Write about a time you were hurt.' We aren't scoring how many sentences were about being hurt, we're scoring the quality of the writing. His descriptive elaboration of Sadie? That's what we're looking for."

Organic Writing Is Always Healthy

We use prompts four times a year for the specific purpose of having a common conversation across our elementary schools and for collaborative scoring opportunities. Every year I get requests for more prompts, lists of prompts, and books of prompts. I use this story to explain why I don't believe that's the answer. Once I was coaching in a classroom on a hot day. I was observing the teacher when a fuzzy little friend popped in through the open door and ran across the room. The children squealed and picked up their feet as a squirrel, obviously confused, dashed about, trying to re-trace his steps to get outside. He scurried up the pillows in the quiet corner and ran behind the "Top Ten Ways to Grow a Reader" poster. Eventually the teacher and I persuaded him to go outside, and the kids named him Nutty.

A little later, after the students returned from lunch, the teacher turned on the overhead and said, "This is Dental Awareness Week, so today we'll write about, If you were a toothbrush, what kind would you be and why?"

My mouth dropped open. When a squirrel named Nutty comes into your classroom, there is no better gift for a community of writers. Imagine the writing that might have come from that opportunity!

I encourage teachers to have students choose topics from shared experiences, personal journal entries, wonderings, science observations, and any other writing that arises organically. The salt, pepper, and everyday spices are teaching them to write because they have something important to say. Prompts are fine every once in awhile. But like the use of smoked paprika, we shouldn't overdo it.

Which prompts seem to get most kids writing? Here are some we've liked:

- Write about a time you were hurt (emotionally, physically) or a time when you almost got hurt but didn't.
- Write about something you know or something you can do.
- Write a letter to persuade your teacher or family member to make a change.

How do you give kids leverage to make a prompt their own? Here are some supports:

- Read mentor texts related to the topic.
- Let them talk and brainstorm with others.
- Turn the prompt around if necessary.

Consider These Questions

Do you know teachers who overprompt? What student needs does it meet? How often do you think prompting is appropriate? How much organic writing is happening in comparison?

No More Flying Pigs

It was spring when I met with Leslie. She had invited me to her classroom to try out some problem solving with her students. She was in her fifth year of teaching. Her first graders sat in rows doing math worksheets, and it was quiet.

I did a demonstration lesson, and afterward, we discussed it. She was excited to record the types of questions I posed for the kids, because she wanted to get better at her own questioning strategies.

"While I have you here," she said, "can I ask you about writing?"

I still had fifteen minutes before my next meeting, so I said, "Of course."

"Well, we have one of those prompt wheels," she told me. "You know—the kind that you spin three different circles and it gives you a new combination of a prompt? There are hundreds of different ones so you never run out."

"I'm not familiar with that," I said. "What is the prompt you came up with?"

"That's what I wanted to talk about, because I'm just feeling a little bit worried that it won't appeal to my first graders. It ended up being 'Tell the story of what would happen if a flying pig lived in the apartment upstairs.'"

"I'm sorry?" I blurted.

"Tell the story of what would happen if a flying pig lived in the apartment upstairs," she said.

"Oh." After a moment I regained my composure.

Then she chuckled. "It sounds even more ridiculous when I say it out loud."

I laughed too. "I'll admit I've never heard that one before."

I kept a straight face when I asked, "Do you think the kids have experience to draw on to write about flying pigs?"

She grinned openly. "No, totally not. I don't even think all of them have experienced a real pig."

"And what about having an apartment upstairs? Do they have experiences with apartment life?"

She shook her head.

"Would you want to write about flying pigs in an apartment upstairs?" I asked her.

"Not at all. I think my story would be cheesy. I think I need to go back to my team and say I don't want to take the time to write to that prompt. Can you help me pick a different one?"

Even before I got back to the office, there was an email from her in my inbox.

"I can't believe I was even considering that prompt! OMG—thanks for saving me from the flying pigs."

"That's my job," I replied.

She sent me back a winking smile.

Not-So-Bad Prompts

Vicki Spandel was the first author who convinced me that the search for great prompts is pointless. There are perhaps only two kinds of prompts out there: the *just bad* prompts and the *not-so-bad* prompts.

Along with other teacher-leaders, I seek out not-so-bad prompts that have multiple entry points. For example, working with a group of teachers, we wanted our third graders to convey a real experience in writing. Together we brainstormed a list of picture books as mentor texts and noticed the strong feelings that came through the work. We created this simple prompt: *Write about a time you felt _____.* Further, we created a lesson guide for teachers that included:

- time for read-alouds of mentor texts,
- modeling of writing,
- brainstorming a list of feelings, and
- storytelling with partners (or the whole class) to get ideas rolling before we asked them to pick up their pencils.

The results were encouraging. A sad paper here about big sisters who are bossy. A mad paper there about a best friend who moved away. A happy paper about going to Vegas with Grandma. One of our favorites was a scared paper about getting stung by a Portuguese man-of-war in "Moka-pea." When a student wrote about feeling lonely that very day because of something that had happened on the playground, it got me thinking about what might have happened if we teachers had filled in that blank and asked him to write about his favorite day. He may have refused that prompt because he didn't feel happy at all. All kids have feelings, and we provided multiple ways for them to show us their best third-grade writing.

Putting Prompts in Their Place

I presented on "Writing Across the Curriculum" to several audiences with the big idea of promoting nonfiction writing in all of the content areas.

"In addition to the district prompts, how often should students be responding to a prompt?" a fourth-grade teacher asked.

The room got a little quiet when I responded, "As little as possible."

"What do you mean?" she asked.

"I would suggest that we overprompt kids. Let your students write about field trips and letters to the guest speaker. Have them write to Marcus before he leaves for Mexico. Let them write for the parent newsletter. When they have real audiences and real reasons to write, they'll give us their best stuff. On-demand writing to a prompt is one of many skills and is no more important than all the other types of writing."

After that relatively unpopular statement a couple of the quieter teachers emailed me. One said, "Thank you for putting prompts in their place. I am going to do a monthly classroom newsletter written by kids, and now I feel like I have the words to explain why to my team. I'll still do some on-demand writing but probably only for the four times a year we collaboratively score."

Coach As a Mirror

Do you work with teachers like Leslie, the first-grade teacher with the prompt wheel? It's easy to understand why prompts are so inviting. You can prepare your lesson plans days, weeks, even months in advance. Prompts are safe and tidy. One assumption is that it eases the prewriting process because students don't have to self-select topics. Yet I find that the teachers who request lists of prompts from me also tend to ask me what to do with the resistant writers in their classrooms.

One said to me, "Yesterday I asked them to write the story of a rock. Any rock! Just tell about what happens. And they just sat there."

"Like a rock?" I wanted to ask.

I am comfortable sharing my own experiences with prompts and how I've come to the realization that many young writers are overprompted and undermotivated. Yet my job as a coach is also to be a mirror. The simple act of listening to Leslie read her prompt out loud helped her hear it with new ears. I asked her questions about her writers' experience, and then I asked her to walk in their shoes. By reflecting, she realized that that prompt wasn't what she wanted for her writers.

Further, if students aren't responding well to a prompt for those fifteen minutes a day, what better use might we make of that time? If we saved up those seventy-five minutes each week, what could we have kids do that real writers do? I wonder . . .

Consider These Questions

What are some examples of how on-demand writing is useful in life outside school?

What is the value of using a prompt?

How often do students really need to do prompts?

Which prompts seem to get all writers connected to something they can elaborate on? Boys? Girls? Students with limited life experiences? Student new to English?

What is the cost of overprompting?

Prewriting Is a Party!

"Does anyone here like parties?"

The fourth-grade classroom where I'm demonstrating a lesson is a forest of tall, standing arms. *Everybody* likes parties.

"That's what I thought. So I'm getting ready to have a party, and I wondered if you could help me plan. What are some things I might need to think about for my party?"

"Are you going to have balloons?" asked one student.

"Oh, I need to think about decorations," I said.

"You'd need a list of who you are inviting," said another student.

"Are you going to have a theme for your party?" asked a third.

"What a good start. I want to make sure we come back to the idea of a theme for my party. Now turn to a partner, go back and forth, and make a list on your think pad of party-planning ideas. You have two minutes."

Purpose

Parties are an engaging way to ignite discussion about prewriting with writers of all ages. Even (and maybe especially) in upper-elementary classrooms, some students think of prewriting as something teachers make you do for school writing. Because I want kids to view school writing as authentic writing, I want them to know three things:

- there is a purpose for prewriting,
- it can take many different forms to fit the writer's style, and
- there are times that prewriting isn't necessary at all.

What is the purpose of a party plan? A plan keeps track of the details, helps organize a sequence of things to do, and shows how the parts fit together in the whole "theme." We plan writing for the very same reasons.

Not all parties are planned. After a soccer game, players meet for banana splits and end up at the goalie's house for a sleepover. Sure, they don't have pajamas or a toothbrush, but spontaneous parties are a lot of fun. Good writing can happen that way too.

Planning Writing

After the fourth graders connected prewriting and parties, we made a list of all the different ways they plan their writing. Here's what they came up with:

1. We talk to someone else about everything that comes to mind.
2. We use a taxonomy* or an organizer for everything that comes to mind on the topic.
3. We freewrite, just start writing. And we go back to our journals for ideas.
4. We cluster.
5. We go someplace quiet and think.
6. We draw pictures!
7. We ask questions.
   * An alphabetic taxonomy is an organizer for kids to brainstorm words and phrases that start with letters of the alphabet (the letters A–Z are written down the side) about their story.

At age ten, these writers already have experienced at least seven different savvy ways to start their writing. The extrovert probably likes to talk about the topic for a while. The visual student loves to draw pictures and add details there first before starting the text. I often start freewriting and then go back after a few minutes and "mine" my good ideas for a cluster.

Although I believe it's essential to be able to use more than one of these strategies to stretch ourselves as prewriters, I also believe that prewriting can sometimes be a barrier for some writers. I found one such student with a Justin Bieber haircut and glasses (new to the class I was working in) staring at his paper and biting his lip. Some oddly shaped boxes were drawn on his paper, and writing had been erased. He looked like he was about ready to cry.

"What's going on?" I asked him.

"I don't know how to do the prewrite for this," he said.

"What do you know how to do?" I asked.

"I just want to start writing," he said.

"So just start writing."

"Really?" he asked. Really.

There will be a time and place for learning prewriting strategies, but for now let him write.

Clustering

Clustering is one type of prewriting strategy that I teach explicitly to kids after we've established the purpose for prewriting. Here's an excerpt from a transcript for how I introduced it:

"Now that we know why we plan parties or writing, I'm going to teach you a strategy you may have already used in one way or another called clustering. What do you think of when you hear that word? Tell your partner."

Students brought up things like peanut-chocolate clusters, some had heard of cluster bombs or of star clusters, and some mentioned the pods or clusters of classrooms.

"All of these are connections to clusters," I said. "A peanut-chocolate cluster is a group or a cluster of peanuts held together with chocolate. Star clusters are a cluster or group of stars. When I hear *cluster*, I think of a cluster of grapes. Draw a cluster of grapes in the air for me. Yes, I can see that there are many different grapes coming off a stem and going in different directions. So that's what my prewrite for my writing is going to look like too. I'm going to model a cluster of a story that really happened to me when I was young.

"I'm going to do the first part of planning my story by talking to you about it, and then I'll invite you to retell my story. Let's start. When I was young, I was short, and I wasn't that great at a lot of games on the playground, but I loved tetherball. I would stand in long lines just to get a chance to play once or twice at recess.

"Now, Partner A, retell my story so far to Partner B."

Kids around the room started gesturing about tetherball and long lines. Within thirty seconds, I called them back. I used retelling to make sure kids were accountable for listening and were engaged, but I made sure to keep the amount of retelling short so that we could keep the lesson moving.

"This one day, there was a new rope on the tetherball that was longer than the old one. I had stayed in for several rounds, but this time when the player hit the ball, it smacked me right in the face. Pow! I got a bloody nose. Kids helped me to the nurse's office, and a friend of mine called me Heather Tether, which was sort of sweet and funny and made me smile.

"Now, Partner B, retell the second part of my story to Partner A."

The volume climbed as they re-created my story. I heard "Pows" around the room, and several kids clutched at their noses. In thirty seconds I brought them back with the "attention" signal.

"What else do you wonder about my story?"

One student asked, "What other sports had you tried?" I told him.

Another, small student said, "How much shorter were you than the rest of the kids?" I answered her question too.

A boy wanted to know if I broke my nose. Luckily, no.

"I feel ready now after talking to start my cluster," I said. On a piece of blank paper I wrote "Heather Tether" in the middle. "Part of my cluster will talk about how I got hurt," I said as I drew the first cluster.

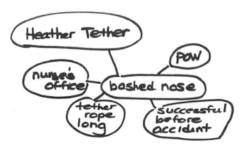

"Another part of my cluster will tell about how I wasn't the best athlete on the playground," I added while they watched.

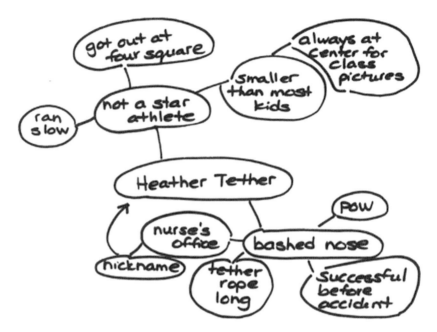

Students in partner teams told each other how I created my cluster. They had a chance to rehearse out loud what they had seen and review what they would be doing next. In the whole group, one student pointed out that my grapes were misshapen.

"I draw my grape outlines around my words, so some look squashed," I said. "I don't know how many grapes I'll need until after I know what I want to say."

Another student commented, "I thought you had to draw them first and then fill them up with ideas."

"Try it and see how it works. Now choose your own idea. Maybe it's related to mine, or it's another one from your notebook. Start playing with this cluster idea. We'll put some of yours up to look at in a few minutes."

Playing with Prewriting

There is something about that word *play* that seems to ease the tension around writing in a classroom. Many times our prewrites are an exercise in thinking and generating ideas—nothing more. I remember one teacher who shook his head in response to my statement, "I've never really considered that prewriting didn't have to be developed, yet I do that all the time with brainstorm lists."

Recently in a fourth-grade class, the teacher and I noted this variety of prewrites that students selected independently:

Eleven students clustered.

Six students created a storyline. A storyline has three boxes for
beginning, middle, and end with space for brief text.

Five students listed their ideas.

Three students drew pictures and labeled them.

Only two students had no prewrite at all.

With our data, it's a healthy sign that students are prewriting on their own
and selecting from a variety of prewrites that match their needs. Party on!

Consider These Questions

How do your students begin writing? What would your "How We
Start" list have on it?

Do students see you using your own writing to model prewriting?

How often are students able to play with prewriting without
continuing through the full writing process?

When is prewriting a barrier?

What is the distribution in your classroom of students' self-selected
types of prewrites?

Coaching Reluctant (?) Writers

I'm not sure I've ever met a reluctant writer. Oh, she may look and he may sound reluctant, but they rarely are.

Take, for example, Eduardo. Eduardo slunk into his sixth-grade literacy block every day. He rolled his eyes, put his head on his desk, and often called out, "I'm bored!" Eduardo's teacher was unsure if he was struggling because of his lack of confidence with English (Eduardo comes from a Spanish-speaking home) or just generally disliked reading and writing.

After the morning minilesson, I watched Eduardo lay his head down on top of his journal. Although it appeared to be napping time, it was crafting time.

"What will you write about today?" I bent down next to him so we were eye-to-eye.

"I hate writing," he groaned.

"That sounds like an interesting topic. Have you written about that yet?"

"What?" he asked.

"How much you hate writing?"

He looked up. "I can write about hating writing?"

"Many of the best pieces of writing are about things writers love and hate. How might that start?"

"Uh . . . 'I hate writing'?" he said.

"That would catch my attention. Right to the point. Then what would come next?" I encouraged.

"'I hate writing so much, I'd rather do just about anything else'?"

"Uh huh. Cool. Get that down."

Then I walked away to give him space. He watched me for a while to see if I was serious and then picked up his pencil. According to his teacher, Eduardo wrote more that day than he'd written all year. After he'd been writing for about ten minutes, I read his piece. One of his lines caught my attention: "I've always hated writing."

"Really? You can't remember liking writing?"

"Maybe in like kindergarten and first grade I liked it," he conceded.

"And what was writing like then?" I asked.

"Easy. I could do it."

"When did you stop liking it?"

"When I had to write more than a sentence," he said.

"That's a great anecdote. Do you know what that is?" He shrugged and I continued, "An anecdote is a small related story within a piece of writing. You could add a great piece about liking writing in first grade until you had to write more than a sentence."

Eduardo's façade could fool anyone into thinking he was reluctant, but he wasn't. At the end of the literacy block I wrote him a note that said, "You did great work today. Keep writing, Eduardo." He didn't smile at me, but I watched him take that sticky note and put it inside his journal for safekeeping. I wondered how much positive feedback Eduardo had received on his writing over the years.

Coaching Writers with Wows and Wonders

What do you do poorly? Pick one thing in your life. For me, it would be keeping my refrigerator door clutter-free. My fridge is plastered with a Student of the Month certificate from eight months ago, a rainbow painting, a band schedule, a coupon, a progress report, notes to remember . . . You get the picture. Although I like to say it's the publishing place for my three wonderful kids, I also know it's bad feng shui. I need to reduce the visual clutter in my kitchen.

Now imagine someone on a daily basis reminding you of how poorly you do this thing you've chosen. I imagine a family member saying, "Look at all this visual clutter. You need to do something about this. You need to store the certificate, file the coupon, recycle the progress report. . . ." I don't know about you, but having someone hound me about my weaknesses is not a great motivator.

Yet, in my work with teachers around writing, some have the hardest time finding something nice to say about kids' writing. Every piece of writing offers opportunities to affirm something that a writer is doing well. And that's essential as we build children's identities about themselves as writers. Knowing what we do well gives us inspiration to do more and willingness to look at other things we could improve.

One simple structure we use is Wow and Wonder with student writing. A Wow is one or more things that we can affirm that the writer is doing well. The Wonder is one thing the writer could improve in this piece and subsequent pieces.

Take this piece of second-grade student writing by Maddie:

Der mrs radr
i lit pet the cat be cus I lik the rhyming it is fune an I lik mama pa-
nyas pancakes cas I lkt I'm one step ahead of you I like is r pete is
and pet the cat is fune becas I like I lave my red sos

The same passage with spelling translation:

> Dear Mrs. Rader,
> I like *Pete the Cat* because I like the rhyming. It is funny. And I like
> *Mama Panya's Pancakes* because I like "I'm one step ahead of you."
> I like Pete the Cat. It's funny because I like "I love my red shoes."

There are many Wows I might draw Maddie's attention to in this letter to me. For content, Maddie gave me specific examples of what she likes about the Eric Litwin's and James Dean's (2008) *Pete the Cat*. She liked the rhyming and the refrain "I love my red shoes." She also liked the book I read, *Mama Panya's Pancakes* by Mary and Rich Chamberlin (2005), and remembered the refrain from that book, "I'm one step ahead of you." Real writers elaborate by giving us examples like this. Maddie did that.

A Wow in her conventions is that her words have spaces, and I would guess that she used a chart or the book itself to get down the titles and the refrain, "I'm one step ahead of you." Real writers refer to original texts all the time for correct spelling of titles and quotes.

If I wanted to work on content with Maddie, I Wonder about keeping her details about the books together. In her sequence she gave me a detail about Pete the Cat, then Mama Panya, and back to Pete. Moving that last sentence would increase this piece's organization and clarity. It would also be a lesson that Maddie could apply to other pieces to "group ideas that are alike."

As for a Wonder about her conventions, there are many directions to go here, but I will practice restraint by not going into all of them. In spelling, I notice two high-frequency words—*like* and *because.* I might spend a couple of minutes having Maddie add these to her personal dictionary or discussing how she might use her personal dictionary to support her. Then I'll make a note and check back with her on future pieces, praising her as she spells these words correctly in her writing. I also notice there is no punctuation. I might have Maddie read the letter to me, make notes where she naturally pauses, and show her how to put in punctuation. In either case, I'm going to focus on one small thing she can do to improve this piece and future pieces—one nudge forward as she grows as a writer.

Coaching Teachers of Writing

With each teacher I coach, I learn more about language that instills confidence in teachers and their ability to teach writing.

I asked a teacher, Jen, if I could record our conversation, listened to the voice memo later, and wrote down this question:

> *What are your ideas about how to teach prewriting explicitly so students understand the purpose and use it successfully?*

It's a simple question, but let's break it down further:

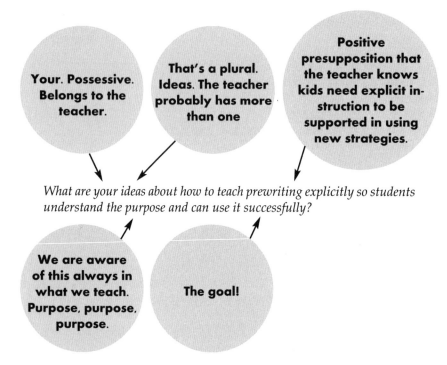

What are your ideas about how to teach prewriting explicitly so students understand the purpose and can use it successfully?

When I show up at a meeting with an open-ended question, trust in the teacher, and the ability to listen, it will trump anything I might "tell" every time.

Consider These Questions

If there were no such thing as reluctant writers, what do you think kids need to be successful in writing?

How often do you notice the Wows of student writing? Have the teachers you collaborate with had explicit practice writing and talking about Wows?

Do you focus in on a small number of Wonders with writers? Have the teachers you collaborate with had explicit practice prioritizing one Wonder?

When you pose questions to educators, do you notice words and phrases that highlight possessives, plurals, positive presupposition, and purpose?

Drafting and Stamina

It was the beginning of triathlon training season. As I slipped into the pool, I was reminding myself of what I knew. Stroke, stroke, stroke, breathe left. Stroke, stroke, stroke, breathe right. Pull the water. Keep your head down. Kick. Harder. After a mere ten lengths in the pool, my arms were tired. How would I ever be able to swim a half mile nonstop for the triathlon?

Although I asked the question, I knew the answer: by building my stamina. Ten lengths the first day is twelve lengths the next week, which is fifteen lengths the next, and at that point I'm doing about a quarter mile: halfway there. When I give myself plenty of time to train, the gains are small and appreciable. A month before the race, the day of ten-length sore arms is only a memory.

Students build stamina in the same way. Stamina in general means "staying power" or "toughness," and those are exactly the qualities needed for writing.

Often when we think of staying power related to writing, we think of the amount of time a person spends writing at one particular sitting. Katie Wood Ray, author of many books—including one of my favorites, *Already Ready* (2008)—talks about another kind of stamina, and that is the staying power to come back to the same piece and pursue projectlike work, connecting one day to the next. A third kind of stamina I address highlights toughness. Every time we reread our work and doctor a word here and a phrase there, we show toughness. Every sentence we cut or move to its rightful place is hard work. Every ending we rewrite is stamina too.

There are three kinds of literacy stamina:

1. One-sitting staying power
2. Same-project staying power
3. Toughness to revise* (this gets a short take of its own)

One-Sitting Staying Power

One-sitting staying power is the type of stamina I see most often taught in classrooms. Thanks to the work of many workshop models such as *The Daily Five* by "The Sisters" Gail Boushey and Joan Moser (2006) that focus on teaching expectations through slow, gradual release, teachers begin by expecting a shorter time on task and increase the time expectation as students' skills strengthen. I got to see one-sitting staying power up close and personal in Linda Karamatic's class, where second graders wrote for almost five minutes on the first day of school. And in April? Those same seven-year-olds wrote for more than an hour as Linda and I taped our Listen In conferring sessions with the Choice Literacy crew!

Another aspect of staying power is knowing when and how to take breaks. I just got up and took a brisk walk around my property because I'd been writing for about twenty minutes. After that short span of time, I find that if I get up, stretch, and move for a couple of minutes, I can come back to my project with renewed energy and work for another twenty or more. Often in those transitions, my good ideas flow. Kids can learn to take appropriate breaks to rest their hands, change position, or browse through a book.

With the second type of stamina, consider this: do students know how to "pick up where they left off"? Some naturally understand project work, but many do not. Students are successful when they have an organized writing system that allows them to locate their current project followed by time to review what they were working on the previous day. Explicit strategies such as "point and chat" with a partner buoy their connections to past work.

Point and Chat

"Welcome back from recess, everyone. I can see your pink cheeks. I'm glad you were running around. Yesterday in writing we started our literary nonfiction pieces. Turn to someone next to you and whisper the topic you are writing about. If you need to peek into your writing folder to remind yourself, that's fine."

The room is filled with whispered topics such as "tigers," "mangoes," "Japan," "polar bears," and more.

"I asked you to bring your writing folders down to the carpet because it can be difficult to know how to start again after your first day of writing. Does everyone remember that I'm writing about rice noodles?"

I show them my writing folder. "I'm going to model with my partner, Felix, and I'm going to 'point and chat' for a minute to tell Felix what I'm working on to help remind myself of where to start. Watch what I point to and listen to what I say. You can tell me afterward."

I point to the note cards in the right-hand pocket of my folder. "OK, Felix, yesterday I found one . . . two . . . three . . . facts about rice noodles and I have two more blank cards, so I could start by finding more facts if I wanted." Then I point to the lined paper. "I also started describing what happens to the dry rice noodles when they are put in warm water. I left off with the word *and*"—I point to the word—"so I could keep writing about that, because I haven't told yet about how they get soft and slimy in the water. I think I'm more excited about the describing part right now, so I'll whisper-read what I've written so far and then add more."

I pause. "What did you see me point and chat about?"

The kids recall me pointing to my facts cards and my lined paper. One student in the back says, "You pointed to your last word to help you remember."

Then Felix models with his folder and points at his note cards. "I worked on facts about mangoes all day yesterday, so I have one . . . two . . . three . . . four . . . five cards. I'm going to keep getting more facts today. I wrote down the website so I could go back there, because it's a really good one. When I get about three more, then I'm going to start on the story part about eating mango on my uncle's farm in California. I have my notes on that right here." He points.

"Now, writers, turn to your partner and point and chat about what you were working on yesterday and what you may work on today," I say. The room is filled with words such as *facts, nonfiction, started, now, today,* and *write*. We review what the voice level in the room will sound like, and then I offer an invitation: "If you are unsure of what you are working on today, stay at the carpet for a moment."

This day four writers stay. One was absent yesterday. Another is unsure if she should keep fact finding or transition to her literary part. A third isn't liking his topic as much as he thought he would. The last just wants to show me what he's got.

I don't make assumptions that kids will know how to start back up with a project. I know I won't need to model "point and chat" every day, but right now they need the support. I also don't assume that every student got what he or she needed during partner talk, so I offer the flexible small group at the carpet. Without that step, in my experience it's sometimes been five, ten, even fifteen minutes before I've found them struggling to get started.

What Happened? What's Next?

One-sitting stamina and project staying power are essential skills for writers. For some, this writerly tenacity comes naturally, but for many others it needs to be modeled, taught, reinforced, and celebrated. When I take teachers to observe in rooms of distinguished teachers, they all comment on the students' level of independence and their stamina. By April it looks like magic, but in the beginning it was a patient investment of intentional teaching.

I'm swimming comfortably in the pool now, and soon it will be time for me to transition to the lake to prepare for my Seattle triathlon. The swim leg of the triathlon is often the most difficult for new triathletes. A half mile may not seem daunting until you are in the water and swimming and swimming and swimming. I'm thankful I've had good friends and coaches to encourage me to build my stamina—it's made all the difference. I'm not fast, but I finish.

Consider These Questions

How long can your students currently sustain writing?

What are some strategies you use to help students connect to projects and continue work?

What does stamina look like in your writers? What do you want it to look like?

Coaching
About the Test

I would encourage anyone nearing testing season to read aloud the picture book *Testing Miss Malarkey* by Judy Finchler with colleagues. Simultaneous laughs and groans erupt at this portrayal of our society's relationship with testing. The story of testing is told from the perspective of a student and begins, "Miss Malarkey is a good teacher. Usually she's really nice. But a couple of weeks ago she started acting a little weird. She started talking about THE TEST: the Instructional Performance Through Understanding test. I think Miss Malarkey said it was called the 'I.P.T.U.' test" (Finchler 2000, 1).

As the story continues, the kids are told the test "isn't that important" and "won't affect your report cards" or "mean extra homework." But they watch the adults around them and Miss Malarkey can't stop biting her nails and the principal loses it over No. 2 pencils with crumbly erasers. The parents attend a PTA meeting and fuss about test anxiety and real estate prices.

This story and the real stories it brings to life remind me that children listen wholly to our melody and attend only slightly to our words. In other words, they watch us to find out the true importance of THE TEST.

Teachers' Approaches

A teacher's approach to testing is as unique as his or her teaching style. I worked with two teachers who were disappointed in their state writing assessment results and took very different approaches.

When I asked Sharon how she taught writing last year, she showed her copied packets of short writing activities and daily journal prompts. I knew that Sharon was a feedback queen. She wrote questions and comments all over the students' papers, and they corrected the papers and handed them back to her. "Plus," she added, "we did several all-day writes to prepare for the test."

Bill had a very different approach. He used a writing workshop model loosely and had his students giving each other peer feedback. The students were very accustomed to writing projects that they collaborated on together. Most of the projects were self-assessed, and he said they were very anxious when test time came around.

123

When we sat down together, I asked, "What do kids need to do to be successful on the statewide writing test?" I took notes as they answered.

- Bill: They need to be able to generate their own topics.
- Sharon: They need to be able to follow the directions of the prompt.
- Bill: They have to care about what they are writing about.
- Sharon: They need to use good conventions.
- Bill: They need to be able to use that checklist to revise.
- Sharon: They need to organize and sequence their ideas.
- Both Bill and Sharon agreed: They need to elaborate.

One by one we went through the list and I asked, "How can we teach kids to [generate topics, follow directions, care, use conventions, revise, organize, and elaborate] *independently* by the spring?"

What Helps?

In the movie *Apollo 13* (1995), an intense space capsule scene near the beginning of the film ends in disaster. Fortunately it turns out to only be a simulator in a virtual reality capsule that helps astronauts and the ground crew prepare for missions. Because astronauts typically have only one chance to complete a task in space, they need to be well practiced before the real thing. In fact, simulation mishaps give them a chance to avoid future disasters or aborted missions.

Although high-stakes testing is not the same as launching a space shuttle, participating in a well-planned simulation can help students prepare for the real thing.

It benefits test takers to know what their materials will look like, what the directions will sound like, how to budget their time, and how to develop stamina for the duration of the test. In our state, fourth graders have an entire day to prewrite, draft, revise, edit, and write a final draft on two separate testing days (one for narrative writing and one for expository writing). A couple of weeks before the test, many teachers stage an "all-day write" to help simulate the testing experience.

Guiding a Simulation

Bill, Sharon, and I planned for guided writing with a continual workshop model flowing from minilesson to independent work time to reflection. Sharon anticipated that the state assessment's writing criteria checklist that was read to the students in the direction phase would be ignored because it was so wordy. During the simulation, we annotated and illustrated the checklist to translate it into words that the writers knew. Then Bill suggested that kids needed to know how to personally respond to the prompt, so we taught a minilesson on how to bring your personal passion to a prompt. "If I love to play touch football" (and a number of the students at their school do), "what might I write about if the prompt is 'Tell a new student about what you like best about school'?" They all agreed I should write about touch football at recess. "If I love animals and the prompt is 'Write about something to improve the school,' what might I write?" The kids thought up how I could write about having animals in the classroom. "Because I'm an expert in touch football or know a lot about animals, I'll be able to bring more to the prompt," I said.

Here is an outline of how we paced our guided all-day write.

First hour:
- Read directions and invite questions
- Annotate writing criteria checklist
- Minilesson: Connecting personal passion to a prompt
- Body break

Second hour:
- Minilesson: Choosing the best prewrite for you
- Time for prewrite and drafting
- Reflection: Share and celebrate variety of prewrites
- Body break

Third hour:
- Minilesson: Stamina for drafting
- Time for drafting
- Reflection: Share catchy leads
- Body break

Fourth hour:
- Minilesson: How to use the checklist as you revise
- Time for revision and editing
- Reflection: Share changes made to draft
- Body break
- Time for writing the final copy

Reflections

Although we anticipated many of the obstacles in an all-day write, we were still surprised. Bill's face drained of color when more than half his class was unsure of what was meant by the word *plot* in the narrative checklist.

I smiled at him and said, "There's still time." The next week we brought out *The Plot Chickens* by Mary Jane and Herm Auch (2009) to give kids a great reminder of plot and to model what good writers do.

Four of Sharon's students finished in the first hour. Three of them were capable but hurried writers who wrote less than a page. As I conferred with them, I said, "With such a short piece, you would be cheating yourself out of a stronger score." All three went back, slowed down, and wrote more elaborated pieces.

Bill said, "I realized that my writers spent so much time cooperating that I hadn't explicitly taught them what they needed to be able to do on their own. I think last year my kids panicked because the situation was so foreign to them and no one could help. Showing them how to transition to this is important."

Sharon admitted, "Even though we did lots of practice writes, I've never done it so intentionally. I think this allowed them to walk through it and ask questions all day long. It surprised me how much fun it was to learn about the test day together."

I don't support teaching *to* the test and stressing kids out, but I do support timely teaching *about* the test in a relaxed manner. One of the last tasks I assign is this: Draw a picture of what you think the person scoring your work will look like. Often I get pictures of robots or squinty-eyed teachers with tightly bound hair. "Would it surprise you that people like me score those tests?" I ask. They gasp, "But you are nice!" "Yes," I say, "and those people scoring, just like me, want you to do your best on THE TEST."

Consider These Questions

How do you relate to Bill and Sharon?

What do your students need to be able to do independently for testing?

What obstacles do you anticipate?

What simulations might help them learn about the test so they can be successful?

How do you differentiate between teaching to the test and teaching about the test?

ERPing in the Classroom

When I go into a classroom to work on revision, I begin by asking the students to answer three simple questions on a half-sheet preassessment. This provides the context for my professional conversation with the teacher and a student-centered approach to looking at the effectiveness of my coaching.

Question 1: Do you like to revise your writing?
I like it_____ It's OK_____ I don't like it

Question 2: When you revise your writing, what do you do?

Question 3: If you had written the following six sentences, what would you revise? Please add, delete, or change as if this was your own writing.
There are many things I like about school. I like recess. I like lunch. I like it when I play with my friends. All in all, I like school.

The first question assesses attitudes; I find most students don't like revision (or at least their perception of revision). The second question looks at the students' procedural knowledge. Many answers are "I look at my writing and I check the spelling." The third question is a performance assessment. Typically in a class of twenty-five or more, few students know how to make changes to content.

ERP

In response to requests from teachers to help their students revise, I developed a process I called ERP. It's not another word for belching—it's a set of steps to get kids to play with revision.

I begin with a sketch of a Chihuahua. Normally, the fact that I cannot draw recognizable animals doesn't come in handy in the classroom, but in this lesson hook, it does. I ask kids to tell a partner what animal they think my drawing represents.

"A fox?" "A bat?" "An elephant?" "A cat?" "A lynx?" "A wolf?" They guess.

After their predictions, I tell them I was attempting to draw a Chihuahua. The more polite students just look at me with pity, and the others laugh. I laugh too.

"What do I need to revise in my picture?" I ask them.

"Make the ears smaller and more pointed."

"Make the eyes bigger."

"I don't think it has whiskers like that."

With a different-color pen, I revise the picture until they are satisfied that it looks much more Chihuahua-like.

"Today we are going to revise our writing just like we revised our Chihuahua," I tell them, "so we can make our message clear to our reader."

The Steps

Briefly, I tell students what the acronym *ERP* stands for and how each of the words has a special meaning.

> *Explicit* means we're going to study exactly how to do it so it's clear.
> *Revision* means to "look again" at our writing.
> *Peers* means we are going to need each other to do this work.

1. Read for one minute. (Hold your hands like a book.)
2. Talk for one minute about possible revisions. (Use your hands to make alligator mouths snapping toward each other.)
3. BOTH partners write for two minutes on sticky notes and then stick them on the writing. (Mime writing.) The writer records ideas for making future revisions. The responder also writes questions and suggestions as a gift to the writer.
4. SWITCH! (Cross arms and point.)

I also give each student a bookmark that lists questions and prompts to help them begin to learn the language of effective response. Many of my bookmarks look specifically at writing traits. For example, the word choice bookmark begins with the statement, "Thank you for sharing your writing" and follows with feedback prompts such as "You repeated the word _____ a lot. What else could you say?" and "What is the exact name of or the specific word for _____?" and "Which words could replace *stuff, things, fun,* and *cool*?"

Teaching the Language of Revision

To put ERP into practice, I ask a student to model the process with me. I have two samples of student writing that students in the class have not authored but are appropriate for the grade level and that scored low on our rubric. Sometimes I write the samples, and sometimes I adapt papers from previous students. Students don't take it personally when they are discussing papers in need of revision that are not their own. As the students become more skilled with the structure, we'll transition to their own writing and gently address "not taking things personally."

Step 1: A student volunteer reads the first piece for one minute. I tell the class that I am listening carefully to the writing so I can ask good questions and make suggestions, because "good revising comes from reading, talking, and writing about what we've written."

Step 2: At the end of the one-minute reading, I have a minute of my own to respond. I start off with my gambit (a canned word or phrase) that begins, "Thank you for sharing your writing." Then I use the bookmark to guide my feedback. The model student and I discuss the paper as a two-way conversation.

Step 3: I model what I would write on my feedback sticky note at the same time my student volunteer writes the ideas she took from our discussion of the writing.

As my partner and I finish modeling, I ask the group, "What did you hear us say and what did you see us do?" for each step.

The Power of Rewriting

In the beginning and training phase, I introduce the concept of revision in a way that is playful (through an animal drawing) but that also provides a useful and memorable analogy that students can hold in their minds as they begin to learn what revision is. When they help me improve my Chihuahua drawing, they are practicing a skill they will later apply in a more difficult context.

In this early phase, I also spend time setting up the procedures (how we will distribute the papers, sticky notes, bookmarks) and behavior expectations (how we give feedback and ask questions in a respectful way). The payoff comes when students have learned to ERP, because they can read, listen, and talk about writing in a structured way, as a warm-up or continued practice, in less than ten minutes.

One student said, "I never liked to write until I learned to ERP." When I asked him why, he said he felt like it gave him the chance to just get his thoughts down in his first draft and they didn't have to be perfect. He knew he'd have the chance to talk with one of his classmates about it and rewrite it later. Sounds like writing as real writers, doesn't it? In my postassessment with the three revision questions, the teachers and I are often amazed by how much students' attitudes toward revision have improved, their ability to distinguish it from editing, and the quality of changes they make to the sample.

A few things to remember about ERP:

- Prepare some short samples of weaker writing to use as models for revision. Transition to the students' own writing once they are comfortable ERPing. You'll need two different samples each time: one for the first partner, and a different one for the second partner.

- Use a bookmark to give a focus for the revision and to support the language development.
- Have plenty of sticky notes and scrap paper on hand.
- Use a timer.
- Keep an anchor chart with the steps, times, and your expectations.
- Monitor partners closely. (I have them stay on the carpet the first few times they ERP so I have proximity.)
- Build on their strengths and give feedback by sharing what you are seeing and hearing in line with ERP.

Consider These Questions

What pre- and postassessments do you use to measure your effectiveness when coaching?

Which classes or students would benefit most from ERP?

What bookmarks or anchor charts do you use to teach the language of talking about revision?

How might teachers "ERP" to experience the process as new learners?

Extreme Makeover: Revision Episode

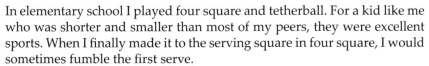

In elementary school I played four square and tetherball. For a kid like me who was shorter and smaller than most of my peers, they were excellent sports. When I finally made it to the serving square in four square, I would sometimes fumble the first serve.

"Do over!" I'd call and repeat for effect. "Do over!"

With my second chance, if I was lucky, that serve would go just where I wanted it: into the back corner of the diagonal square.

We loved do-overs on the playground, but kids don't have the same enthusiasm for do-overs in writing. When I was teaching, I thought maybe it was just *my* students, but now as a literacy coach, I see this is true for many young writers.

The quick preassessments from students leave me with the winning combination of "I don't like it" and "I don't know how to do it." Why is that? When I surveyed more than 200 elementary school teachers, I asked, "What is the most difficult step of the writing process to teach?" The answer was a resounding, "Revision!"

Yes, it is hard, and many of us weren't taught explicit revision strategies. If you asked me to fix up my computer, I would dust off the screen and the keyboard and call it good. I don't know how to get inside and go deeper. No one ever taught me how, so I superficially clean it and hope that's good enough.

For example, my daughter Maya is a strong writer. As I was planning this essay, I asked her if she liked revising. She shrugged. "Well, kids don't really like to be told what to do, and they often like their story just the way it is," she said. "Some kids want to get it over with, and revision seems to take longer. And sometimes I worry that if I change something, it will ruin it."

That sounds about right.

As a young writer, I would ask people to read my writing, but I felt irritated if they had any suggestions for improvement. It's like the last line of Shel Silverstein's poem "Tell Me" from his book *Falling Up* (1986):

131

"Tell me I'm perfect—But tell me the truth."

For me, revision lacked purpose.

What Is Revision?

Revision is often confused with editing. I recall a college professor saying, "Before you turn it in, be sure to 'reviseedit' your work."

Oh yes, that was the term for fixing up your writing: reviseedit. A German word to be sure. To confuse the issue more, an "editor" helps with both revision and editing.

Revising and editing are both processes of looking again at writing and making changes for the better. However, the purpose for each is very different. In *revision* we look at making changes for content, organization, and style. *Editing* is only about conventions. If I make an analogy to getting dressed, revision is changing your pants, shirt, underwear, shoes, and socks. Buttoning your shirt, tucking it in, and zipping up your pants? That's editing. Through editing, we make our writing conform to common conventions, thereby making it easier to understand. Editing is a courtesy to our readers.

Revision is *elaboration* through adding words, phrases, sentences, and paragraphs. It's also *deleting* text to stick to the topic. *Rearranging* text is part of revision too. Each one of these changes results from answering simple questions such as these:

> *What's my point?*
> *Does it fit my audience and purpose?*
> *Is this clear?*
> *Can I say it a better way?*
> *Do I enjoy reading this out loud?*
> *Does it sound like me?*

In addition, it's about an overall understanding of what makes writing good and the assumption that everyone—even a professional—is a better rewriter than prewriter.

Demonstrating Revision Explicitly

Some teachers assign revision: "Be sure to revise." Others hand out a checklist. But even the most beautiful checklist may simply be a place for writers to place checks. Assigning and using a checklist are not the same as *teaching* revision.

Help with teaching revision is one of the top requests I get from teachers when they are working on writing. When I ask, "How does revision currently look in your classroom?" I usually hear one of two scenarios:

Scenario 1: Full release to the kids
"As the kids finish up, I tell them to get together with another person who is finished. The good writers seem to do OK, but the other writers

don't seem to say much beyond 'good job.' They end up wasting a lot of time because I can't be with every pair to coach them."

Scenario 2: No release to the kids
"As the kids are writing, I have a few come up and share their writing with me. I comment on a couple of things and make suggestions. Pretty soon every one is lined up to read me their work and get feedback. There's not enough of me to go around."

One of the questions I ask in my initial meeting with a teacher is, "What is your learning style?" The majority of teachers tell me, "I need to see it—live." Some say they learn from viewing video; some say they learn from reflective conversations; a few say they learn from reading. But most opt for live interaction.

So when I go in to demonstrate teaching revision with a teacher, I make sure he or she has a "watch-for." Here are some examples:

Which writers are making revisions?
What kind?
How do they mark them?
Which writers are not making revisions?
Where might they start?
How do students respond when strong writers in the classroom display
    their revisions?

Before/After Effect

Although I'm not an avid television watcher, I pay enough attention to know about wildly popular shows such as *Extreme Makeover*. Whether the show's focus is weight, plastic surgery, or home remodels for needy families, Americans are fascinated by the before-and-after effect. Oh, the drama in the buildup to the Big Reveal. There's the thin, smiling woman standing in one leg of her old pants. Shock! Disbelief! She's a new person! We love it.

In the spirit of extreme makeovers, I choose a writing sample that needs revision. Sometimes these are samples from other classes with names removed, sometimes they are samples I find online, and sometimes I just make them up.

After reading the paper out loud, I say, "What is this writer doing well?" Every writer does something well, and every writer can use feedback on what to keep.

Then I say, "We are going to give this writing a makeover."

I place the sample on the overhead or under the document camera and grab a green writing utensil. Each student has a copy of the same writing and sharp green pencil. Green is the color of new shoots pushing through the dirt; we aim to make this writing come to life.

Together we talk about the message of the writer, crossing out words and sentences that don't seem to fit. If the lead isn't catchy or the conclusion isn't satisfying, we rewrite them. When we find general words, we replace them with precise ones. We limit needless dialogue and choose a very purposeful exclamation or short exchange. Sometimes we find places where the writer is telling instead of showing, and we help there too.

Then I have a student read the "before" and another read the "after," and we exclaim in shock and disbelief. It doesn't even sound like the same paper!

Now the students take action by pulling out their writing folders. Mighty green pencils begin adding, deleting, and changing their writing. I encourage them, "Let's just play with it and see what happens." I praise, "Look at all that beautiful green on your papers. This is what good writers do."

As they finish, the kids walk to the front of the room and record the types of changes they made by placing sticky notes on the revision chart.

Encouraging Approximation

After lessons like these, the teacher and I look at the revision chart sticky notes. Most writers note they "added description," which is typical. Subtracting from writing is a skill that develops over time. Some specific revisions I've seen from young writers are like Dacia's original sentence: *My dog is very brown, furry and likes to play.* She revised it to say, *My playful dog is a pile of brown furry cuteness.* Although we might not call this revision an extreme makeover, she showed a willingness to make a change to her writing and did something original with language. As another example, Carlos substituted a better word. He'd marked through the word *big*, written *huge* instead, and later added "bigger than a globe" above it. To him, the comparison told the reader more information and better reflected what he wanted to say. He's writing as a real writer.

I don't get discouraged anymore about writers' tendencies to start with superficial revisions. Borrowing a word from Brian Cambourne's work published in *The Reading Teacher* (1995), the students are "approximating." As learners, we stay in the approximation zone for a time before we deepen our understanding. With more practice, I'll use examples like changing *big* to *huge* and I'll pose the question, "Do those revisions give the effect we are looking for? Would everyone know what size you mean?" Because that's what we do as writers. We get an idea, and we put it down word after word. If we can, we put it aside for a day or maybe four, and then we read it again with new eyes. We notice that it's not as clear as it was when we first wrote it, so we work to improve it. Each day we show up to the page a little more confident, a bit more experienced, and a tad more trusting as we take up the green pencil . . . and we write and rewrite.

Consider These Questions

How do you distinguish between revision and editing?
When do you use revision?
What extreme makeovers seem to prompt writers to make their own revisions?
Do you model revision explicitly and often?

Inquiry into Editing

My seven-year-old grows windowsill plants inspired by her botany work at school.

"What do you notice?" her science teacher asks.

Ahna notices the shape of the leaves and the color of the stem.

"What else?"

She measures with a ruler and finds out that the plant is seven centimeters tall.

"What would happen if you put your potato plant in the dark?"

Ahna put the plant in the dark and discovered it didn't grow there.

"Which do you prefer for your plant, light or dark?"

"Light!" Ahna's sure of it.

"Why is that so?"

In science we know that students' discoveries lead to new questions, further investigation, and high engagement, and we can transfer this same inquiry process to conventions of writing.

Inquiry Questions

Jeff Anderson has two books titled *Mechanically Inclined* (2005) and *Everyday Editing* (2007) that changed the way I teach editing. This passage was powerful for my learning:

> *Editing instruction starts with students observing how powerful texts work. What are writers doing? What can we learn from their effectiveness—and, more often than not, their correctness? This way of editing is inquiry based, open-ended and bound by meaning:*
>
> > *What do you notice?*
> > *What else?*
> > *How does it sound when we read it?*
> > *What would change if we removed this or that?*
> > *Which do you prefer? Why? (Anderson 2007, 13)*

You can use these questions from Jeff and some favorite mentor texts to get started with editing inquiry.

Beyond Daily Oral Language

When I inherited my third-grade classroom as a second-year teacher, it came with a DOL book: Daily Oral Language. There were enough incorrect sentences to last the whole year. And that was the idea—post incorrect sentences and then have the students make corrections. Although it was efficient to have ten minutes of my writing time planned each day, I began to notice that it wasn't engaging, nor was it transferring to students' own writing. At all.

After trying DOL for a year, I deemed it an inauthentic writing activity and put the binder on the bookshelf. Kids don't transfer grammar to their own writing this way. Writers study correct grammar, usage, and style to become better writers. We read sentences out loud and listen to the sounds. We notice how a sentence looks. We mimic the masters.

The inquiry process also helped me move from rules to purpose. The rule is that sentences begin with a capital letter but go deeper. Beyond the rules, conventions make sense—they have purpose.

Snapshot from a Primary Classroom

In a second-grade classroom, I tried on my first inquiry lessons with conventions. According to our state standards, second-grade writers should start their sentences with a capital letter and use a capital for proper nouns such as names.

I used this excerpt from *Elephants Cannot Dance!* an Elephant and Piggie book by Mo Willems (2009).

> *Gerald, it does not say that you cannot* try!
> *You are right, Piggie!*
> *I can* try to dance!

This piece was a great choice because it (a) was a favorite in this classroom and (b) provided opportunities to look at the convention of capital letters in multiple ways.

I began with Jeff Anderson's first question: "What do you notice?"

"There are three exclamation points," said Blaine.

"That's true," I said. "I think Mo Willems uses those quite a bit. Why does he use them here?"

"Because Elephant and Piggie are excited," replied Blaine.

"What else?"

"There are slidy words," said Cristina.

"Slidy words?" I asked.

"Yes, *try* and *can* are slidy words."

"Oh," I said. "Yes, those are in italics. Why do you think he did that?"

Cristina didn't know, so she called on Desiree. "Because he wants you to see them. So he makes them," and then Desiree demonstrated by tilting her head to the side.

"What else?"

The kids noticed that the sentences started with capital letters, that everything was spelled correctly, that *try* was used twice.

Then Eduardo took us where I'd been hoping we'd go. "*Gerald* and *Piggie* have capital *G* and capital *P*."

"Why do they have capitals?" I asked.

"Because they are names," Francisca said.

"What would happen if we removed the capitals?" I said. I replaced the *G* with a *g* on a sticky note and the *P* with a *p*. "Now let me read it again."

"It sounds the same," said Gage, shrugging.

"No, it doesn't," protested Henry, "because Piggie could be any piggie, not THE PIGGIE."

"What do you mean, THE PIGGIE?" I asked using his emphasis.

"That's his name, but you don't know it if it isn't a capital."

"These are lowercase letters," I said, and had the kids mirror me and make their palms face together about an inch apart.

"These are uppercase letters," I said, and moved my hands farther apart. "Which one is easier to notice?"

"Big!" they chorused.

"Right! So writers use big letters to get you to pay attention to things like Gerald and Piggie's names because they are important to the story. Which do you prefer? Lowercase or uppercase for names?"

"Piggie with a capital *P*!" summed up Ivy.

Snapshot from an Intermediate Classroom

During a writing class for teachers I led, I shared the power of an inquiry approach to conventions. A teacher I'll call Jessie said, "I'd love to see my sixth graders get that excited about anything to do with writing." I asked her if she would be willing to have me come to her classroom to try some lessons on conventions. I was curious to see if this approach worked just with the younger set or if we could get meaningful dialogue going in a classroom where most grammar instruction was delivered via worksheets.

The first day I read aloud a short passage from Sandra Cisneros's *The House on Mango Street* (1989) to introduce myself. During planning, Jessie and I looked at student writing. I noticed and commented that most of their sentences were simple sentences and that any embedded elaboration was done with parenthesis instead of other ways to set off the information.

"It makes me think about introducing appositives," I said.

"Say what?" Jessie asked.

An *appositive* is a noun or a noun phrase adjacent to another noun that adds essential information. For more information, Grammar Girl elaborates on appositives at http://grammar.quickanddirtytips.com/appositives .aspx.

I showed Jessie that "uses commas in appositives" was in our punctuation standards for sixth graders.

"I guess I ignored it because I didn't know what it meant," she admitted.

Looking through *The House on Mango Street*, I was delighted to see that Cisneros is generous with her use of appositives.

"They are all over the place!" commented Jessie. "Now I won't be able to help but notice them."

I used this single sentence from the book as our mentor text: "And inside it would have real stairs, not hallway stairs, but stairs inside like the houses on T.V."

The next day I opened up with the million-dollar question, "What do you notice?"

The sixth graders were slow to start. One mentioned it started with a capital, another noticed that TV had periods, and a third pointed out that the sentence starts with *And*.

I read it again. "What else?"

"There are commas," Kasey said.

"What are they doing?" I asked.

"They are . . . ," Kasey paused, "sitting there?"

"What would happen if I removed (comma) not hallway stairs (comma) but stairs?" I read the sentence like this: "And inside it would have real stairs inside like the houses on T.V."

The kids were quiet, thinking.

Leanna ventured, "Now you don't know they aren't hallway stairs."

"Yes, that's true. Is that important in the sentence?"

Most kids shook their heads, but Mason said, "I think it is, because she's saying that there are a certain kind of stairs she wants."

"What does that even mean, anyway—stairs like the houses on TV?" a student asked.

The kids started chattering. They said there were stairs that had banisters rather than hallway walls on both sides and that they were places to film dramatic scenes.

Mason said, "It's like they are rich stairs, not stairs just to get upstairs."

"And which sentence do you prefer?" I asked. The majority of the students liked the original sentence. Jessie was smiling as she took notes on her students' thoughtful dialogue.

"Sandra Cisneros uses appositives in her writing. The two commas set off the information 'not hallway stairs' to contrast it with the TV stairs. It's something good writers do to add more information right there in the sentence. I'm going to write *appositives* up on the chart paper, and when you are reading today, see if you can find some examples. Tomorrow we'll try writing some together."

My seven-minute minilesson was complete.

What Happened? What's Next?

Tentative would be the word to describe how I started designing inquiry-based conventions lessons. I worked to find the just-right skill to go with the just-right text. It was important for me to start that way, but it wasn't sustainable over time. Now I see an issue with one or more students, grab a couple of books off my shelf, and head out to demonstrate or coteach with those questions in mind. It doesn't matter whether I'm teaching capitalization or appositives, kids learn how to look at the texts they read as writers and even more specifically as writers with editors' eyes.

Consider These Questions

Who does most of the talking during lessons on conventions?
Do the "lessons learned" transfer to student writing?
Do your students notice conventions on a daily or weekly basis?
If you've not used the inquiry approach, which convention topic and mentor texts might you use?
What resources do you need to move forward with confidence?

Coaching Editing

Not long ago I was crafting an email and struggling with one particular sentence. Was it grammatically incorrect or just awkward and in need of revision? *What's more important?* I asked myself. *Do I get the invitation out before the workday is over, or do I fret about one gangly sentence?* And so I sent the e-mail. Five minutes later I got a call from an email recipient and teacher I'd never met.

"I'd love to take part in the opportunity described in the email," she said. "It sounds like it's perfect for me."

"Great," I said, "and thanks for calling right away."

"Sure. I was calling, though, because I'm an English teacher, and there is a sentence that just needs to be fixed. I'm not even sure what's wrong with it, but it's extremely awkward. I had to reread it twice to get your meaning. You really ought to change it."

"Thanks," I gulped. "I'll see what I can do."

Although I was blushing from the chastisement on the other end of the line, I had empathy for Ms. Grammar. When I'm sitting in a class or a meeting and an error is made, I have to focus on not focusing on the mistake. For example, one teacher-leader I work with frequently uses the verb *elicit*, but when she includes it in documents, she writes it as *illicit* (which makes the phrase *the teacher will illicit conversation* . . . interesting). Another friend uses *effect* when she means *affect*; a third colleague mispronounces many multisyllabic words such as *discombobulate*, which comes out as discom-bobble-you-late.

I do have my own issues. Admittedly I can't spell *diarrhea* or *occasion* without spell-check or quickly recall when to use *who* or *whom* or *lay* versus *lie*. Style guides and Grammar Girl blogs help me out, but I think many of us sometimes feel insecure about our hold on written and spoken English. That's important to keep in mind.

To Correct or Not to Correct?

A coach in another district once asked me if she should correct a collaborating teacher on her misspellings on the board.

"What are you coaching her on?" I asked.

"Mostly setting up rules and procedures," she replied.

"Do the errors get in the way of the kids' understanding of rules and procedures?" I asked.

"No," she said.

"Would you want her, early in your coaching relationship, to feel insecure about her spelling instead of focusing on setting up rules and procedures?"

"Definitely not," she said.

"It seems like you could correct it in your transcription if you are taking notes on what was written on the board, but perhaps wait until there is an invitation. There have been many great writers and teachers who are notoriously bad spellers. Since that's not the focus of your work, maybe there will be another opportunity."

A month later at a meeting, the coach thanked me for my advice and explained, "Now that we've built a relationship, she's admitted to me that she struggles as a speller, feels embarrassed about it, and wants to work on it. I suggested an electronic dictionary next to the board, and she's going to try it. I think if I would've said something earlier, she might never have opened up."

Independent Editors Need Scaffolding

Although I might not correct a teacher's grammar or misspellings, it is our job to help students learn to edit. Notice that I didn't say it's my job to simply correct students' errors. No, it's my job to help them grow as independent editors through my teaching. One approach corrects a single paper, whereas the other approach has the potential to help every future paper.

A first-year teacher I'll call Kendra stayed after writing class one day to talk to me. In tears, she shared how she didn't have a life anymore. "I'm going home at six o'clock and then staying up late to correct papers!" she said. She showed me her rolling cart packed with a stack of journals and file folders with three different writing assignments.

I invited her to show me some of her fifth graders' work. She opened a file folder and took out student writing marked up with her editor's marks in purple pen.

"Are these going to be published?" I asked.

"No," she said. "Why?"

"It seems like they could be doing the editing themselves. It doesn't have to be perfect."

We talked for almost an hour that day. She explained how she didn't feel comfortable leaving the mistakes on the page. She thought parents would think she didn't have high expectations.

"If you don't feel balance in your own life with the ways things are, let me ask you this: are the kids learning from all your editing?" I asked.

"No," she said. "That's the thing. They just keep making the same mistakes, and I keep marking them."

Marginal Writing

We took one of her papers and I showed her how to use a technique I call "marginal writing." Marginal writing uses tallies in the margins to indicate to students that there is a convention error in that line that needs their attention to find and fix. It shifts the work of an editor to the student. Similar to "error analysis" in mathematics the message to a learner is, There is an error here and you are capable of finding it, fixing it, and learning from your mistakes. This is what good writers do. Special thanks to my daughter Maya for letting me use a fifth-grade persuasive paper she wrote as a sample.

> ll Do I think a tax on candy is
> l   right? yes! why? Because a percent
>   of the taxes is going to health care
>   reform. For my family we pay about
> l   20 dollers for a doctor visit because
> l   we have health care. Other familys
> l   have to pay hundreds of dollers or
>   more. So they don't go to the doctor,
> SF   don't take care of themselves which
> consider
> revising they should.

In the example above you can see a variety of convention errors, from missing capital letters in short sentences ("Yes! Why?") to the misspellings of *dollers* (dollars), a usage issue with *is* instead of *are*, and an incorrect attempt at making *family* plural. Although there is an error in almost every line, these convention errors do not prevent us from making meaning of this passage. You can also see that I've noted *SF*, which stands for "sentence fluency," to indicate to the writer to work on restructuring the sentence *So they don't go to the doctor, don't take care of themselves which they should.* With a simple transition and rewording, this sentence might be revised to say, *When health care is so expensive, some families don't go to the doctor to get the care they need.*

The point is, who should do this work? If I am scaffolding young writers to learn to be independent editors as they mature in their writing, I can't rescue them by making their corrections and asking them to recopy. I can give them small passages and feedback to "find and fix" some editing issues. The writer of this paper would catch some of these quickly, and other errors would require rereading and a bit of word study. A little struggle and perseverance strengthens editors.

The marginal writing feedback, I've found, is most effective when applied in small doses. For a student who struggles with conventions, I might tally only the first few lines, leaving fewer than ten corrections for the student to make. With a writer in control of conventions, I might look at the whole piece. In effect, both students may have about the same amount of editing to do and it doesn't become overwhelming. I also encourage students to talk to each other. The "Ask three, then me" rule works well here: ask three other students about the editing issue, and if you can't find it or understand why it needs correction, then ask me.

Prioritizing a Focus

In my short take called "Coaching Reluctant (?) Writers," I discussed the use of Wows and Wonders with feedback to writers. Writers need to hear what they are doing well with conventions. A Wow might be, "I noticed the way you used all caps in your use of the word *SOMEONE* to emphasize the voice. It helps me as the reader." And then choose one teaching point for your Wonder with conventions. "I also noticed that in the verbs *coming* and *staring* you forgot to drop the *e* and add the *-ing*, spelling them *comeing* and *stareing*. I've made a note to look at your verbs in your next pieces. You can add, 'Drop *e*' and 'Add *-ing*' to your crafting notes."

When I met with Kendra two weeks later, she said she was doing better, but still editing much of her students' writing with her purple pen. She'd looked at the standards and was feeling panicked about everything they had to know.

"What is expected of the writers?" I asked.

She pulled out our writing plan with the conventions expectations for fifth graders. Capitalization rules, punctuation rules, mature spelling, paragraphing—it was all there.

"But where," I said, "does it say that students at standard are doing all this, all the time on every paper? You are looking for evidence of these skills in their writing, but not all of it all the time."

Kendra took a breath and considered what she'd need to do to narrow her focus. Looking through the student work, we made a list of seven possible issues to focus on with her fifth graders:

- Lack of paragraphing
- Verb tense confusion
- Subject/verb agreement
- Fragments
- Run-together sentences
- Forgotten commas
- Incorrect punctuation of dialogue

We decided that forgotten commas were less worrisome than verb tense confusion, which was less prominent than run-together sentences. Kendra planned whole-group minilessons to draw attention to run-together sentences in writing, and then we discussed how she'd follow up with small groups and individual conferences.

"It's so much better to look at the work and pick one thing at a time than to try to address all those standards in every paper as their editor," Kendra reflected.

Consider These Questions

What grammar insecurities do you have?

When is it appropriate to correct a colleague's misspelling or grammatical errors?

Who does the work of editing?

How do you/could you use marginal-writing feedback instead of editing and having students recopy?

How do/might you use Wows and Wonders with conventions?

How do you prioritize a focus on conventions?

From "Cute" to "Dude, I Told You": Rubrics, Exemplars, and Anchors

How to Look at Student Work

The Superpower of Reflecting

Assessing What Matters

From "Cute" to "Dude, I Told You": Rubrics, Exemplars, and Anchors

"It has to be proficient, because it's just so cute," the teacher across from me said. She admired the illustration and reread the catchy lead out loud. There were four of us at the table scoring second-grade writing. One nodded and shrugged, and the other looked at me.

"We could look at the anchor set to see if there is a good match," I suggested. As we looked through the set, we found a similar paper in the two range (below standard) on a six-point scale. Although there was a catchy lead in this paper, it showed little creativity in ideas, cluttered organization, and sentences with problems. Using our rubric and anchors, this "cute" paper was not yet proficient.

When the male teacher read his paper aloud next, the same teacher said, "That is really cute. I say give it a four."

"Hmm," I said. "Let's look at the anchor set and see if there are any matches."

One teacher read the rubric at a level five and thought the paper might score there. When we looked at the anchors, we did indeed find a high five that matched well.

The process continued through our scoring session, and I learned that this teacher used *cute* to mean, "Wow, isn't it amazing the effort that these kids put into their writing?" I was in full agreement. All of them were cute papers by that definition. However, several pieces were not proficient yet, and having clarity on how kids are doing so that we can help them grow is essential.

Rubric Cheerleader

In my early years of teaching, I was a rubric cheerleader. I loved writing rubrics, annotating them with my students, and using them for student and teacher assessment. I'm using the word *rubric* generally here to mean a scoring tool based on a set of criteria (usually district or state standards) that describes different levels of performance. I could use rubrics to communicate to students and families before a task so it would be very transparent what I would be scoring on and what was valued in the work. Often I would have students use the rubric to score themselves and compare it with my score.

What I didn't know then that I understand a little better now is the limitations of rubrics. Rubrics can define levels of quality, but even with a six-point rubric there is a range of quality within each level. In addition, an evaluator has to take a "best-fit" approach with a rubric. We found this to be true with the scoring team I described above. For example, there was no indication of where to put a seven-page paper with great ideas and organization in the first two pages and the pure repetition of those great ideas in the next five pages. Further, rubrics will say things like "writer elaborates" or "writer states his/her position on the issue." The definition of what it means for a second grader to "elaborate" or how a sixth grader "states a position" is not part of the rubric. The work of defining comes through the art of scoring and using exemplars or anchors.

If we were talking about an exemplary student, we would be discussing one who works hard, follows the rules, and is successful. In the same way, an "exemplar" is a model that is worthy of imitation. For students, exemplars serve as targets. For scoring purposes, having exemplars moves the conversation among educators deeper because we can define what it means to elaborate or state a position. We can gather actual student work and stake a claim: "This student is elaborating; this is what it looks like." In the same way, having nonexamples also helps move the conversation, making a statement: "This student is not elaborating; this is not there yet." We call packets of student work that include exemplars and not-yet exemplars our anchor papers: examples of student work that serve to help evaluate others' work. Like an anchor, they hold the boat steady in choppy water.

Even the youngest students use rubrics informally. You can say to a classroom of kindergartners, "Think about ice cream. Show me three fingers up if it's one of your favorite foods, two fingers up if you sort of like it, or one finger up if you don't like it." Many classrooms have noise-control posters or agreements that are rubrics: "Remember we use a level-two voice in the hallway." With examples, they get what the difference is between each level, and as their understanding increases, so does their ability to evaluate their own or others' performance.

Colleagues have different opinions about when and how often to use rubrics, but most agree that communicating criteria clearly and giving examples helps students be successful.

After a teacher and I have our criteria set on a rubric, we have students annotate and interact with it and practice using it before they ever rely on it to judge their own performance. Simply handing out a rubric does not help most students interpret the scoring information.

Demonstrating with Rubrics

"In front of you is a rubric, and there are four numbers on the left. You can highlight those numbers. A rubric has sentences that describe what work looks like at each of the levels. As I read you the sentences for a level one, notice and highlight words and phrases that seem to be repeated."

I read descriptors for level one. "What did you notice was repeated?" I ask.

"There were some *no* this or *no* that," says one student.

"Some *nots* and *little*," says another.

I nod. "I agree. Let's annotate or note *little* or *no* to the side. A paper at this level will need to be revised to work up to a two."

I read descriptors for level two.

"What did you notice that was repeated?" I ask.

"On this one, I saw *sometimes* and *attempt*," says a student.

We continue in this way, highlighting words and annotating phrases: *some* and *mostly there* and *consistently meets*.

When we are finished, I have the kids turn to a partner and each share a level of the rubric and some describing words.

Then I pass out or visually display two pieces of student work. "One of these pieces is stronger than the other," I say. "It's up to you and your partner to select the one that is stronger and use the sentences in the rubric to say why you think so."

In the beginning I choose papers that are more obviously weak or strong. Early success with a rubric helps students feel confident as we move forward.

Students read and discuss the papers, and then we come back together as a whole group. As student pairs share which paper they thought was stronger, I constantly take them back to the rubric with questions such as, "What is your evidence from the rubric? Which sentence from the rubric fits with what you said?"

By having students see and hear the levels of criteria, highlight, annotate important words and phrases, and then interact with the rubric through scoring, we begin the conversation of what high quality means for that particular task or project.

Making Rubrics a Part of Instruction

I was observing in a colleague's sixth-grade classroom. After greeting her students, she began to read a sample piece. From the back of the room I could see the kids start to fidget. Two particular boys caught my attention as they flashed what at first appeared to be gang signs back and forth.

When she finished reading, the teacher took off her glasses. "What did you think?"

The students all flashed her numbers. One boy shook four fingers to the side like a fan and then added a stylish one with the other hand. She smiled. "Well done. Most of you see this paper as a five. It was scored a five."

"Dude," said the boy to his friend, "I told you!"

Using rubrics with exemplars or anchor papers serves to give clarity about high expectations and the difference between levels of criteria. Well-communicated tools demystify why tasks get scored the way they do. All students deserve "dude-I-told-you" scoring confidence, which must come from educators who quickly move beyond "cute."

Consider These Questions

For which subjects or projects do you have high-quality rubrics?

How do students learn about those rubrics?

What exemplars or anchors do you have that illustrate the rubrics?

Do you have a process to find agreement with colleagues on the samples?

What do you see your students doing and saying that shows their depth of understanding around scoring?

What Is the Evidence?

The first and most brutal fact that must be confronted in creating PLCs (Professional Learning Communities) *is that the task is not merely challenging: it is daunting. It is disingenuous to suggest that transformation will be easy or to present it with a rosy optimism that obscures the inevitable turmoil ahead.*

–DuFour, DuFour, Eaker, and Many, 2006

Betty had just finished explaining to her team that the student's problem-solving task in front of them was not proficient even though her colleagues scored it a three out of a possible four points.

The other team members looked uncomfortable. Betty was the most outspoken in the group (the leader), and they were quiet. "What are you using as evidence when you say it's not proficient?" I asked Betty.

"Well, for starters, the answer is wrong and he's only used a sentence to explain."

I looked at the rubric. At level three, or proficient, it said the following:

Student reads problem, pulls out numbers and reasonable operation
Computes with accuracy, though some errors may occur
Explains with math appropriate language, but may not be concise
Satisfies requirements of the problem
Answers may be correct or reasonable

"Where in the rubric do you see that a wrong answer is not proficient or writing has to be longer than a sentence?" I inquired.

"Well, it's not written like that, according to the rubric. But I can't allow a wrong answer to be proficient—I have high standards," said Betty.

It's not that Betty doesn't comprehend the rubric or appreciate her team; she just believes her standards trump the agreed-upon grade-level rubric. The way she stays in her comfort zone is to say, "I have high standards." No one can or will argue that point. For teachers who have been isolated for most of their careers during the teaching day, this is an understandable response. Researchers, John Gunn and Bruce King in their article *Trouble in Paradise* (2003) have found this to be true as well. They found teaching teams were often contradictory and complex, with stubborn hierarchies, silenced members and individualistic tendencies.

Gunn and King note "individualistic tendencies" and the complex work of teacher teams that goes under the microscope when collaboratively studying and scoring student work. No longer does the "you do what you do and I do what I do" function, because we have to agree on (a) a common measure, (b) how to calibrate ourselves to score, and (c) collaborative approaches in what comes next for instruction. This means that we need to have common language and values in alignment. Needless to say, it can make for some contentious meetings.

Would It Be Possible?

If you got your teaching degree thirty years ago, you may have been expected to emphasize product, not process. Answers mattered most. Students sat in rows. You ran "dittos" and knew the ins and outs of teaching manuals. Or not. If you got your teaching degree fifteen years ago, you may have been expected to emphasize process and deemphasize product. Answers didn't matter as much as the thinking. Students sat in groups. You may have been expected to create thematic units and used constructivist teaching principles. Or not. Our training, our student teaching supervisor, and the predominant "school of thought" was foundational for our values, and those values may vary widely among colleagues.

Today we know that mathematicians need to be able to problem-solve in unique situations, and this is valued over plugging numbers into formulas without understanding. It matters less what writing looks like on the page and more what the content expresses. Readers need to be thinking about what they read instead of simply word-calling during popcorn reading. Does that mean basic facts, conventions, and decoding are not important? Absolutely not. They just have a place in a bigger picture of what it means to be a mathematician, a writer, and a reader. And that picture is evolving.

As a participant in Betty's meeting, I was processing a lot of information. I knew that her less-experienced teammates were frustrated with the way she overrode their collaborative decisions. You could see it in their body language. You could hear it in their silence. It was also crucial for Betty to have control. If she felt challenged or defensive, things could really unravel.

"Coming to agreement can be difficult with any team of four professionals," I began. "If we scored according to the rubric, can you see how this task could score a three?"

She nodded slightly. "Yes, because the rubric says the answer doesn't have to be correct, it just has to be reasonable."

"So the rubric represents a value of reasonableness with minor errors. Do you think if you handed this back to the student that he could fix it and get a correct answer?" I asked.

"Probably," she agreed. "He's a smart kid—he just made a mistake. But he needs to look more closely and check his work."

Aha, I thought. "Rechecking is such an important skill. Would it possible to score this task a three and add a note to the student to recheck the answer and report back to you?" I suggested.

"I suppose," she said and wrote a 3 on the sticky note. The group took a collective breath.

No Small Thing

Watching teacher teams in my district for years makes me appreciate the complexity and dynamics that go into effective collaboration. In the beginning of our work around Professional Learning Communities there seemed to be an equation like this:

> *Put teachers in a group + Have them bring student work = Increased collaboration and Improved student learning*

But the truth is that that equation worked in about 15 percent of the teams I saw. What I found was that those teams with trust, respect for each other's teaching, a dedication to problem solving, similar values, natural curiosity, and strong communication skills were successful. The other 85 percent were stuck having conversations like Betty's team and wishing they could just go back to doing their own thing.

In some situations an outside facilitator, like a coach, can help in these ways:

Step 1: Confirm that teaming is hard. Because it is. This is no small thing. Encourage groups to establish and write down norms of collaboration, and ask, "What will you agree to do if these are/aren't followed?"

Step 2: Establish what teachers are using as evidence to build common language and understanding within the group. When one or more group members are using different evidence or ignoring the agreed-upon measure, address it gently and clearly.

Step 3: Listen, listen, listen.

Step 4: Paraphrase and take an inquiry stance.
"If we . . . then could . . .?"
"What if?"
"Would it be possible?"

Step 5: Encourage teams to celebrate success. Teams that play together stay together.

Consider These Questions

When you read the opening quote, what came up for you?

What "individual tendencies" like Betty's get in the way of successful collaboration?

How can your language as a leader make or break an experience collaborating with a team?

What steps would you add that work well for you?

How to Look at Student Work

"And there she goes . . ."

My daughter Ahna is officially a bike rider. I'm sentimental about it, because she's the last Rader kid to learn. What's unique about this time around is that she's the first one to learn without me holding the back of the seat and running behind. The new approach since the last time I coached a bike rider is "hands-off" as far as a parent is concerned. You begin by removing pedals and lowering the seat so you can watch kids push off with their feet. This is called "scooting," and it's essential to learning balance. When the rider is scooting for long segments, the pedals go back on.

In the instructional video I watched, the cycling expert gave me things to look for and tips on what to introduce next. For example, instead of running along behind and holding the seat (which doesn't allow kids to learn balance for themselves), I was to watch when Ahna was able to scoot with legs lifted up for a count of ten. Once she could do that, it was my task to see if she was able to look up ahead instead of focus on her feet.

How great it is to know what to watch for and what I might do next, I thought. I connected to a workshop I co-presented called "Looking at Student Work Through Instruction-Colored Glasses" in which we constructed what to watch for and what to do next, using student work to guide instruction.

Who Needs the Feedback?

When looking at student work through instruction-colored glasses, the first thing I consider is who needs the feedback about this work. Consider the following student work that fits into different feedback categories:

Type of student work	Who needs the feedback?
Assessment screener on computer	Special education team, principal, teacher
Writing prompt (1 of 4 throughout year)	Professional Learning Community*, principal, parents, student, teacher
Math postassessment in geometry	PLC, parents, student, teacher
Reader Inventory one-on-one	Teacher, perhaps parents
Science-observation writing notebook check	Parents, student, teacher
Summary preassessment	PLC, teacher

*Many districts use PLC or data-team time to share student data and use a protocol or set of steps to analyze the data. Our district has about eighteen early-release days a year to focus on student work.

Taking the time to stop and consider who needs the feedback can help teachers and literacy leaders make decisions about what form the feedback will take. For example, a principal may request an Excel spreadsheet with *above standard, at-standard, near standard,* and *far below* indicated. However, my PLC will want me to bring the original student work to spread out. Most tasks that students complete won't be analyzed in depth, so I choose carefully. Scoring and analyzing a quarterly formative piece of student writing gives me information to share with my principal and PLC. It also gives me feedback to share with students during conferring as well as with families during conference time. My in-depth analysis benefits both my instruction and my communication with multiple parties.

What Does the Student Know?

For a preassessment, fourth graders summarized a short passage from Nic Bishop's well-crafted nonfiction book *Frogs*. Although the following two students aren't writing a proficient summary yet, these samples tell a lot about what they already know about summaries.

> This story was about nonfiction book that tells you
> about frogs frogs eat moths, beetles, and crickets.
> they also eat 5,000 insects every summer their
> mouth are big so they can get like 10 insects at
> frogs hids among leaves on the rain forest floor
> in south America.

This student has a beginning idea that a summary should be shorter than the original text. She also includes evidence from the original text when she writes, "5,000 insects every summer." I'll be able to help this student understand that summaries don't involve opinions or coming up with a creative analysis like she does when she writes, "their mouths are big so they can get like 10 insects." The original text does not support this statement. A big idea in summaries is that it's about what the author of the piece thinks is important. From this one piece, I know a lot about how to proceed with this learner.

> Frogs wanted to eat but it takes a lot of
> efort so they make up teknecs.

> Someone/frogs
> wanted/to eat
> but/it takes a lot of efert.
> so/they make up tekneks,

The text reads, "Frogs wanted to eat, but it takes a lot of effort so they make up techniques."

If you are familiar with Kylene Beers's book *When Kids Can't Read: What Teachers Can Do* (2003), you'll recognize this student's strategy of "Somebody Wanted But So" which can be an effective frame for summarizing narrative text. If you think about most narrative text there is "somebody" (a character) who "wanted" something (motivation), "but" (conflict), and "so" something happened (resolution). I often use the "Three Little Pigs" as an example. The pigs (somebody) *wanted* to build a house for safety, *but* the wolf wanted to eat them, *so* they had to devise a plan to get rid of him.

The student who produced Sample 2 obviously understands that summaries are shorter than the original text, and she understands how to distill information. I'll be able to help this student learn when to use this narrative frame as well as a rule-based strategy for summarizing informational text.

Beginning with a strengths-based approach, I'm gathering information about what my students already know and making plans to build from there.

What's Trendy?

Before I'm even halfway through the pile of summaries, I'm seeing a trend that fourth graders are including personal information and commentary, which do not belong in a summary of informational text. This is an obstacle I will need to address. Depending on how rooted the misconception or misapplication is, I may have to tackle this in many ways and for many days. I anticipated this because I've been fascinated by the complexity of teaching summarization for a few years, and this pattern is typical of students before instruction. Knowing my students' trends helps me plan for instruction. Although I knew I'd be instructing on the attributes of a high-quality summary, the student work indicates that I may need to spend extra time on the point of excluding personal information.

I'm thinking about the student work on three levels:

- What are trends for the whole group?
- What are trends for small groups?
- What are anomalies for individual students?

With this set of papers, I sorted five preassessments with summaries almost as long as the original text. It's a small trend, but a trend nonetheless. Devoting a substantial portion of class time to teaching that summaries are shorter than the original text wouldn't be useful, because most of the kids already know this attribute. In a small group of these five students, I can share several summaries and have them notice, talk about, and explore how they are shorter than the original text.

Sample 2 represents an anomaly. No other student used the Somebody Wants But So narrative summary frame. I will address that with the student individually with my strength- and curiosity-based Wow/Wonder approach: "I read your summary and I was impressed that you really understand how to summarize narrative texts with characters, conflicts and solutions. (Wow) Nonfiction informational text like the piece from *Frogs* is organized around main ideas and details, so using Somebody Wants But So isn't the best tool for this text. Learning to use the right tool for the right text is part of summarizing. Let's write the question, *What kind of text am I summarizing?* in your writer's notebook as a reminder to think about which tool will work best." (Wonder)

Instruction-Colored Glasses

Because I'm not going to analyze all of my student work deeply, I need to be choosy about the pieces I select. Most of the tasks I find highly valuable have students "doing the discipline." If I'm assessing elaboration in student writing, I analyze independently generated student writing. If I'm looking at high-quality observations in science, I want to examine independently generated scientific observations. When I wanted to consider summaries? I looked at independently generated summaries. Careful, critical tasks that involve doing the discipline give me the information I need. Just like my cycling daughter, I'm not needed to run along behind and keep her from falling. I'm needed to stand back and watch for what she needs next.

Once I select a task or assessment, I take a strengths-based approach and note all the things students already know how to do. This assures me that I won't be repeating information they already know in my instruction, and helps me to understand their current thinking. When I begin to look at the ways the work doesn't meet standard, or the obstacles, I think about it in terms of trends of the majority, trends of small groups, and anomalies for individuals. This way of looking at student work colors the glasses through which I view instruction. The majority trends will be addressed in the whole group, whereas the smaller issues will be looked at in flexible groups, and the anomalies by individuals. The strategies I use for instruction match the needs.

Looking at student work for me has evolved far past "who gets it" and "who doesn't." In-depth analysis on my own, or preferably with a partner or team, leads me to know what I can skip in whole-group instruction, which areas need more emphasis, topics for small-group instruction, individual student needs, and how I want to capture my feedback beyond my personal needs for instruction.

Only one week after learning to ride, Ahna was already doing tricks. Once she had her balance and her ability to brake, she was deciding what she needed to do next.

Consider These Questions

Which pieces of student work do double, triple, and even quadruple duty in giving feedback to interested parties?

If a colleague says, "Why look at preassessments? Students don't know anything; that's why we're teaching," how might you respond?

What trends are you seeing in student work? How will you address them with the whole group, small groups, and in individual conferring?

Transitioning to Guide on the Side

"I want to move more of my professional development from sage on the stage to guide on the side," I wrote as my goal for the coming year. For three years I'd taught classes for teachers that involved my close reading, studying, and preparing engaging activities for an audience. It took ample time and care. Almost always teachers were pleased and got new ideas, but when I thought of the saying *The ones doing the work are the ones doing the learning*, I knew something needed to change.

Who brings the professional development? I asked myself as I surveyed my box packed with mentor texts, student samples, lesson plans, and videos. I do. *What would happen if teachers brought the professional development? What would that look like?*

Bring It

Often during my writing professional development I would hear about young writers. "Jarrod is my fifth grader who can't put two sentences together," one teacher would say. "All of my first graders are writing. They don't really have problems with anything," another would add. *Hmm*, I thought. The way to find out how writers were really striving and thriving was to have teachers bring student work. Instead of talking about what we thought writers were doing, and speaking in generalities, we could look at what they were actually writing independently and talk specifics. These were the specifics that could make a difference in instruction the next day.

Twice during the year for all grade levels, and three times that year for fourth-grade teachers (the shepherds of the state test), we came together for three hours for a collaborative scoring workshop. The teachers brought student writing based on a lesson plan that had been cowritten with teacher-leaders. For example, kindergarten through sixth-grade students wrote *expert* pieces for the purpose of informing another student about something they knew or something they could do. I got first-person reports from my daughters about the prompt:

"I wrote about what I'm an expert on today," said my seven-year-old.

"What did you choose?" I asked.

157

"Writing. And I used details like 'sharpened pencil' and 'regular lined paper,' and I said it was important to have a 'catchy lead.' Do you think that was good?"

"I'm sure it was. You do know a lot about writing."

"I did cooking," said my sixth grader, Maya. Together we watch the Food Network while we work out at the YMCA on the elliptical orbiters.

"That's perfect for you," I said.

Teachers bring the expert writing; I bring the rubrics, anchor sets, and facilitation. Together we will do the thinking and talking about student work, but they will be leading it.

I carefully chose the title "Scoring for Understanding" for the workshops because I wanted to emphasize that the process is much more than assigning a score. The point in taking the time to look closely at student writing is not the number we write on the sticky note, but the feedback we craft and the instruction that follows to meet students' needs: the understanding.

Doing to Learn

The workshop pacing for "Scoring for Understanding" looks like this:

Hour 1
:10 Welcome and logistics
:05 Purpose setting
:10 Consider scoring biases, talk with teammates about personal bias
:10 Talk through each level of the rubric, annotate with key words
:15 Read student samples (anchor papers) at each level of the rubric, discuss
:10 Break

Hour 2
:60 Read aloud and score aloud in teams, facilitators move around room

Hour 3
:45 Some teams continue to read aloud and score aloud; others move to silent scoring
:15 Collecting data on exit slips. How did writers do? What trends did we see?

Be Impeccable

Even though the teachers brought the bulk of the work of the professional development, there is a need for facilitation, and my choice of words needs to be impeccable. This is a new and vulnerable place for many teachers: their teaching is suddenly spread all over the table for others to see.

"Everyone has a bias," I begin. "When we score writing, our job is to be aware of and responsible for that bias." I offer up different biases that teachers have shared over the years:

Topical Bias: Teacher doesn't like or has little schema for the topic and examples.

I often elaborate by sharing how I have to monitor my bias when I'm reading papers about video games.

Student Bias: A teacher's feelings related to a particular writer.

I say, "This might be the best piece of writing your student has ever written. It may be the worst. Either way, if it's a three, it's a three. How you feel about a student's effort or behavior shouldn't affect the score."

Prompt Bias: A teacher's feeling that the student is "off prompt."

We use prompts to give teachers a common subject to score, not as a way to "mark kids down" when they take their writing in a unique direction. The wide-open prompt is simply the starting place to guide the purpose, form, and audience for the writer. We use the question, Can you tell the student read the prompt? to guide us. If a second-grade student writes about how much she loves her dog, we can infer that she read the prompt and that because she loves her dog, she considers herself a dog expert.

Humor Bias: We tend to inflate scores when students make us laugh.

If I've read ten papers and a student makes me laugh by sharing that he's an expert on annoying people, I have to be careful to stick to my rubric and anchors instead of letting the voice of the piece overwhelm other considerations.

Conventions Bias: How it looks versus how it sounds.

Unless we are specifically scoring for conventions, we have to score the writer's message and the content, not the lowercase *I*'s or the lack of punctuation or the fact that she spelled *nephew* "nifyou."

Illustrations Bias: Illustrations enhance, not supplant writing.

In primary papers, we can use the illustrations to help enhance the message, but at times I've found that cute pictures have a tendency to inflate scores.

Drift Bias: Be aware of boredom.

The twentieth paper (or the fiftieth) deserves to be scored with the freshness of the first paper. I encourage teachers to take frequent breaks, move around, and trade papers with each other so they don't "drift" away from high-quality scoring.

Teachers write their personal bias down to share with colleagues and hold themselves accountable for being aware of and sensitive to how it might affect scoring.

Along with considering our biases, we have different norms for a workshop. This is one of the slides I use to guide my introduction:

We agree to . . .
- read papers as if the parent of that student is in the room,
- skip the disclaimer for each paper,
- listen to each other's scoring reasoning and return to the rubric and the anchors as evidence, and
- focus on the feedback to the writers.

I explain *skip the disclaimer* in this way: "From time to time we all have the student who walks in ready to write the next best seller. As teachers we tend not to take credit for his work, and we start into a disclaimer. Or we have a student who writes like a beginner or is new to English. Or a student who has been diagnosed with this or that, or a child who has no parent support. We may say, 'Now, before we read this paper, I should tell you . . .' And although these things may affect writers—and some to a great degree—they shouldn't affect our scores. There is a place for every writer on our continuum today. We want to give them as authentic of a score for this snapshot of their writing as possible, so that we can plan what to do next to help them grow. So feel free to skip the disclaimer."

What Do You See?

As the teachers start scoring in their grade-level teams, I move about, answering questions and discussing papers. During the first few workshops as teachers handed me papers, I read them, consulted the anchor set, and then shared my best-fit score. Again, I caught myself: *Who was doing the work?*

Now it sounds more like this:

"Heather, we got two different scores on this paper. Will you read it?"

I read. I consult the anchor papers and get a score in my head, which I don't share.

"OK," I say. "Which anchor papers did you find that were a close match?"

They find their anchor set.

One says, "Three-B."

The other says, "Four-A."

"And what is your reasoning behind it?" I ask.

"I thought it was like the three because it was still listy."

"I thought there was evidence of elaboration, which pushed it up into the four category."

I nod. "The way I saw this paper was between a three and a four, so you are right on track. The question is, Is that elaboration stronger than the highest three? Can we call it proficient?"

The first teacher says, "Well, now that I see it that way, I guess it is stronger."

"Go with a four?" they double-check.
I say, "Good call," and move on.

Reflection

I've facilitated more than thirty scoring workshops for teachers and one for our principals. The setup was minimal on my part as I watched the focus of our professional development walk through the door in red folders and ziplock bags, in purses and totes. It was demanding work to be "on" to facilitate groups and help everyone leave with reliable and valid scored papers, but I wasn't standing up front as the sage on the stage. I was leaning, sitting, even crouching next to teachers puzzling over student writing. Even after the workshop, teachers would email me or call to collaborate around their papers. I've journeyed to guide on the side and discovered I prefer doing the work by not doing the work. And paradoxically, that's hard work!

Consider These Questions

In what ways are you the sage on the stage? When is this role
essential in professional development?
Who is doing the work in your professional-development offerings?
What are some ways you can move to guide at the side with the way
you structure your professional development?
How does your language move you to sage or guide?

The Superpower of Reflecting

What is your superpower? Are you a great listener, storyteller, misconception spotter, advocator, or feedback giver? Educators have a multitude of superpowers, and we'll focus here on one that takes teachers from good to great: reflection.

Let's first consider if you are a Pollyanna or Eeyore reflector. If you are a Pollyanna reflector, you might find yourself commenting about your lessons like this:

> *"They all learned it so well!"*
> *"Every single one of them understood it completely!"*
> *"I can't imagine it could get any better!"*

Pollyanna, of course, is the character who frames everything in a positive light. It's important for us all to have a little bit of Pollyanna inside of us, especially when our jobs require so much patience and understanding. However, the Pollyanna perspective doesn't help one get better at teaching if everything is always "super."

On the other hand, if you don't relate to this at all, you might find yourself saying things like this about your lessons:

> *"Nobody learned anything."*
> *"Students aren't where they should be."*
> *"There is nothing from this lesson I'd want to keep."*

From the Hundred Acre Wood comes Eeyore, who takes the sky-is-falling-but-it–will-probably-hit-only-me stance. Eeyore finds places for improvement, but he finds them everywhere and is never content.

Depending on whether you lean toward the Pollyanna or the Eeyore side of things, you may need to consider different strategies to move yourself forward. The ideal is to have a balance between the two: to see the good in your instruction (and celebrate it) and the places for improvement (and troubleshoot them).

162

What to Consider

When feeling overwhelmed by the number of points to consider in your lessons, workshops, and units, it's helpful to set some limits in the beginning. There are five basic elements: planning, the teaching event itself, immediate impressions, longer-term reflection, and the changes we make. Here is a list that may provide points for reflection. It is by no means exhaustive, but it may be a starting point. Choose two or three points of inquiry. Note that if much of your work is in professional development, you can consider the word *students* as your adult learners in the questions below.

Lesson objective—Did you state it in the beginning of the lesson? Did you connect its purpose to other learning and life? Is it too broad, as in, *We will write an effective essay?* Think of all the components that go into an effective essay. Is it too narrow, as in, *We will use active verbs in our writing about animals?*

Lesson standard—If someone walked in and asked the majority of your students what they were learning and why, would they be able to answer? Is there a place they could look in the room to find the answer? Is it connected to your standards?

Lesson introduction—Did you get the students' attention? Were you thoughtful about combining their interests and needs with the standard? Within the first ten minutes of the lesson, was the focus clear?

Lesson anticipation—Was any preassessment used (student work, anecdotal notes, or other data) to plan for instruction? What did you anticipate would go well? What did you anticipate as a challenge? Were you correct?

Lesson engagement—Did you think about attention span and create shifts about every ten minutes (or less, depending on the age of your students) to have students talk about, write about, and think about what they are learning? Was there time for individual and cooperative learning?

Lesson materials—Were students able to access what they needed to be successful? Did some students need different materials?

Lesson grouping—What did you offer to the whole group? If you did a minilesson, was it a minilesson or a maxilesson? What did you offer to small groups? How did that meet their needs? What did you offer to individuals? Who did you not reach with your instruction today?

Lesson differentiation—What did you do to meet the needs of your learners? Your visual learners? Your kinesthetic learners? Your students with different learning needs?

Lesson authenticity—At what points of the lesson were students "doing the discipline" with careful, critical independent reading or thoughtful, generative independent writing?

Lesson management—If someone had been transcribing your talk, would it have sounded proactive or reactive? Was there natural movement and transition during the lesson?

Lesson strategies—What strategies did you use to address the content and process needs?

Lesson pacing—Did you hear students saying, "Wait"? Was their work incomplete? Did you have students saying, "What's next?" Did they have some time at the end without clear tasks?

Lesson closure—In what ways did you have students analyze, evaluate, or reflect on the day's lesson? What did you do in the last five to eight minutes to capitalize on their rise in attention span?

Lesson assessment—Besides your perspective, what pieces of evidence do you have to support what students now know and can do?

Coach Yourself

Even if you have a coach, cooperating teacher, or team to debrief with, you are most often going to be reflecting alone. It's a good thing reflection is portable. Most teachers tell me it rarely happens during planning time, and most often happens on a run, during a shower, or, unfortunately, in the middle of the night. So you are going to need to coach yourself. Some teachers I work with tell me they can hear my voice encouraging and questioning when they teach and reflect. It's a great practice to find someone in your life who is both kind and discerning, and to use them as your guide. You can insert his or her name in the blanks below:

What would _____ remind me that was really strong in that lesson? What evidence would he/she point to?

_____ might encourage me to look at this aspect of my teaching. He/she might gently wonder about . . .

As we begin to choose aspects of our work that we want to improve, we want to take the Goldilocks approach. Choose too many things to change and it's overwhelming. Choose too few and it can seem like there isn't momentum. Choosing the right amount is something only you can determine.

Make Time

Each of us has a unique way to reflect. Some, like me, choose to write it down. I have a notebook in my purse as well as a file on my computer so that I can write down a string of questions and thoughts. Here's a sample from a recent workshop for teachers I hosted:

Why didn't more than half of the participants choose to use the template to plan? Did I need to do the model on a piece of poster paper so everyone could see it? How might I revise this time to make it more useful?

Our closure time was cut short. What might I condense earlier in the morning to allow for more focus on math writing?

If writing is not your thing, set up a camera and capture video of whole-group, small-group, or individual conferring. Watch short chunks with your reflective questions in mind. Or ask another colleague to transcribe a portion of your lesson, recording what is said and done. Read through the lesson while keeping in mind one or two things you are watching for.

Many of us reflect with others throughout the day: at lunch, after school, during planning. It can also be powerful to set up a scheduled time with someone to focus on instructional conversations by phone or in person. I frequently ask my colleagues, husband, and friends if I can have fifteen minutes to debrief about a situation that is perplexing to me. If they listen and paraphrase back to me, I can get myself to a new place of thinking.

When we hear the word *reflection* and think of a mirror, that's part of it. We want to see ourselves clearly in the way our work is reflected. But the purpose of reflecting is to validate what we are doing well, so we are likely to continue doing it and to make changes to continuously grow—something we can appreciate about our profession. We have job security in that the work is never done.

We often think of superpowers as something inhuman—something far beyond the capability of mere mortals—but I say the superpower of reflection makes us more human. As one of my colleagues says, "I'm a work in progress." We all are.

Consider These Questions

Do you have more of a Pollyanna or Eeyore stance?
Which of these reflection questions applies in your current work?
How do you make time for reflection? Is it enough?

Coaching Monkey

As a kid, Curious George was my hero. Sometimes I had to cover my eyes when he was about to get into trouble, but I knew in the end he'd do something to make it right. He always did. Although I was definitely not a rule breaker, I secretly shared George's curiosity. With more courage, I too would've folded up those newspapers into boats and sent them floating down the river. It tickles me to think that perhaps my coaching motto, "Stay Curious," comes from my early learning with George.

It's that time again—my evaluation time. As an instructional coach, the evidence and measures for my evaluation are different from when I was a classroom teacher. I'm curious. What is it like for a member of Generation Y in her first year of teaching to work with me? And what's it like for a boomer about to retire? I'm interested in trends. What do I need to keep doing? Where do I need to grow? Hearing from teachers clamoring to collaborate and more resistant colleagues is equally important to me. As the ever-curious coach, I've gathered feedback over the years from the teachers I coach in different ways.

Paper and Pencil

My first feedback from the teachers I worked with as a first- and second-year coach came through two questions I asked on a simple paper-and-pencil survey.

> *What, if any, impact did coaching have on your teaching and students' learning? Give a specific example.*

> *What is your advice for me as I strive to improve?*

Teachers sent their anonymous responses to me through the district mail, but as survey after survey came back, there was no advice on improving. One wrote, "I want to be helpful here, but I don't know what more I could've asked for." And then it clicked. The majority of the teachers had never worked with an instructional coach before. They had nothing to compare me with other than "It's so much better than trying to do this all by myself." I was going to need to find advice for improvements in other ways.

Checkback

In my third year of coaching, I became interested in sustainability. Although I could see significant changes in the short term with teachers, I wondered if those changes would be sustained over time. Would Sharon continue to use problem-solving tasks and increase the students' math dialogue? Would Matt continue to pursue the workshop model for writing after doing whole-group instruction only for ten years? I decided to ask.

Three teachers worked with me for about four to six weeks to improve writing instruction. We co-planned, observed one another (using release time), debriefed, and then scored student work and planned future instruction. At the end of October I emailed each one:

What was the most significant change you have made this fall in your teaching that you've seen affect student writing?

What will that look like in May?

Aria replied, "What I learned was to limit the overwhelming amount of feedback I give to writers. I've changed now to notice one thing the writer is doing well (even the tough papers) and one thing to improve upon. I would hope that I'm still doing that in May!"

Beth replied, "I learned to be less rigid about writing to prompts and to open it up to include their passions. By May I would think that my students would know how to write to a prompt when needed, but more importantly how to generate a topic they are excited about."

Kelly replied, "I have learned better ways to use writing samples and shorter, more focused writing times."

At the end of April, I had a reminder in my calendar to reconnect with the team. I reminded each one that I had promised to follow up. I posed this question to Aria:

From your perspective have you continued to use the "find one thing the writer is doing well and one thing to improve on" in your instruction? How might this have affected the quality and/or attitudes of student writing?

She replied, "I can't believe I went so long thinking that if I corrected them enough that they'd get it. I've seen my students be so much more willing to write when they knew they'd get some positive feedback and only one thing to concentrate on to improve. In past years, we were all overwhelmed and students rarely made revisions because we didn't know where to start. I have a group of the most confident writers I've ever taught, but I know that's because they have a more confident teacher. Coaching gave me that."

Holistic

My interest has expanded to asking many questions about time, resources, my behaviors, expectations, effectiveness, and more. Encouraged by my colleague Becky Lee, I monkeyed up a coaching survey. A week before my evaluation, I sent an email to the thirteen colleagues I'd coached with this year. I gave them the link to the survey and a deadline and then offered to compensate them for their time by leading a lesson or read-aloud while they planned. It's a hard time of year to ask for "a little something more" from teachers, so I wanted to be very respectful of their time. Ten teachers replied by the deadline, and everyone told me it was a very efficient survey and didn't take too much time.

Here is a double-entry journal where I explain my thinking behind the survey question in the right-hand column.

Survey Question	Curiosities
How much instructional coaching have you accessed? Very little (for example, emails, one meeting) A few times (for example, emails, meetings) Often (for example, classroom time, meetings, classes) Continuous (for example, contact throughout the year)	I wanted to see if the way I saw teachers accessing time was the same way they saw it.
The amount of time I spent working with Heather . . . seemed like it was too little; she wasn't available. seemed like the right amount for what I needed. seemed like too much.	Even with a full coaching schedule, I really focus on being available when teachers need me. I wanted to see if my "wish" was their reality.
What were the reasons you accessed a coach? Opportunity to grow as a teacher Learn a new structure or strategy Collaborate with a colleague My principal encouraged me Help with accountability for professional goals Improve classroom management Improve student learning Curiosity to see what coaching was about Assigned because of my program	I'm looking for trends here. Why do most teachers access a coach (in their opinion)?

In which ways do you access Heather as a coach? Check as many as apply.
By email
By office phone
By cell
Attended after-school professional development
Attended meetings with team or staff
Scheduled time in your classroom

With this question I was hoping to see a variety. By using a number of different ways to connect, teachers can go with their most comfortable mode of communication.

What types of instructional support have you received?
Heather demonstrated in my classroom or a colleague's classroom and I observed.
I co-created a plan before instruction with Heather.
Heather and I debriefed a lesson after instruction.
Heather typed a transcript of my instruction.
Heather sent me requested resources (mentor texts, lessons, articles, etc.).
Heather observed me teach and gave feedback.
Heather helped me edit or revise lesson/unit plans.
Heather used video to capture my instruction.
I analyzed or scored student work with Heather present.

With all the different ways to collaborate, I was really hoping that this would show variety.

I wanted to make room for supports I hadn't considered that may have been effective.

Were there other ways not listed that you received instructional support?

In my initial meetings with teachers, I really want to be sure I'm proactively putting this information out there. This was a question to hold myself accountable.

Which of the following topics did Heather discuss with you about coaching?
Confidentiality
Building relationships (trust between teacher and coach)
Common experiences in coaching
Purpose of coaching in our district
Options for what the coaching model could look like
Expectations for teacher and coach

Using the phrases, "Before coaching I used to . . ." and "After coaching I . . ." comment on a shift that you've had as a result of coaching.

This open-ended response question gave great data.

Which areas were expanded after working with Heather?
Writing
Reading
Math
Science
Social Studies
Social Skills
Classroom Management
Other

This was another accountability piece to see how I was distributing my time among the many topics elementary teachers teach.

If you brought a problem or concern to Heather, did she . . .
act like she already had the answer?
ask questions to understand better?
listen closely?
help you find your own answer?
say, "I don't know. Let me get back to you"?

Can you tell this is one of my professional goals? I wanted to find out if this year I'd progressed on using questioning to help teachers be reflective and answer their own questions.

What is Heather's level of follow-through for what she says she'll do?
Strong (She almost always does what she says.)
Fair (She mostly does what she says.)
Poor (She doesn't do what she says she'll do.)

I believe follow-through is a huge component of trust building. I wanted to see if I was living up to my expectations.

Coaching improves student learning.
When I read this statement, I . . .
Strongly agree Agree Disagree Strongly disagree

This is the reason I have a job, so I always want to check in with how teachers see coaching related to improving student learning.

Share a specific example from your classroom that supports your claim.

Another open-ended question to get at the evidence teachers are using.

Who does the work during a coaching cycle?
All me.
Mostly me, with a little of Heather's support.
It's an equitable collaboration.
Mostly Heather; it was only slightly different from having her teach.
All Heather.

My last curious question to see if the way I see coaching responsibility is the same way that my colleagues view it.

What else would you like to add?

More room for those gems that I haven't asked for specifically.

Coaching Data *Is* Student Work

To make a sound assessment, we use multiple points of data. When receiving feedback on my effectiveness as a coach, I consider feedback from my professional-development classes (program-specific data), individual responses from teachers about coaching (teacher-centered data), *and* student work. Diane Sweeney got me reinvigorated about using student work in relationship to coaching effectiveness in her book *Student-Centered Coaching* (2011).

A middle school teacher began working with me to support his students' growing independence as readers. George questioned whether his students were really choosing "just-right" books. The only experience they'd had was relying on external measures like computer tests that generated a grade-level-equivalent reading level. Before we started our work, he gave the students a short survey to answer:

- How confident do you feel choosing a "just-right" book?
- What is the title of a "just-right" book for you currently?
- What are some of the questions you ask yourself when choosing a book?

We looked at their responses during our initial meeting. Although many students rated themselves as very confident, most either said they "asked no questions" or "asked themselves if the grade level was the right one." With the goal of independence, and considering that the majority of texts out there have no printed reading level or colored dot on the spine, we knew this was an important focus for our work.

Four weeks later we'd taught lessons on questions readers ask to determine a "just-right" book, assessed using running records, and conferred with students on better-fit books. George gave them the same survey again, and we used it in our final meeting to talk about our effect on student learning. Working with George was a joy, and he said he had learned a lot. But more than that, we had the apples-to-apples student data in front of us that showed that as a result of our work, kids were asking themselves questions about their background knowledge, their interests, the genres they liked, and more. We also knew specifically which books they were reading and why they had chosen them. With the pre- and postassessments side by side, we were able to celebrate our collaboration and plan the next steps.

Consider These Questions

How might feedback on your professional goals come through your survey?

Which questions resonated with you?

What have you always wanted to know about your coaching?

If the number of respondents has been an issue in the past, how might you increase participation?

What types of student data do you collect to support effectiveness
toward improving student learning?

Where do you get most of your data on coaching right now: from
program-specific, teacher-centered, or student-centered sources?
What is the balance?

Postscript:
An Attitude of Gratitude

My first grader, Ahna, secretly stuck a note in my purse:

"I hope you have an extcnt day Mom. Spis!"
(Translation: I hope you have an excellent day, Mom. Surprise!)

Ahna's blossom of kindness was in stark contrast to my inbox with an email that began, "I thought you'd want to know what my whole class didn't like about the lesson you wrote up." Sigh. Indeed we are in the "Januaries."

In the spirit of paying it forward, I pulled out my collection of thank-you cards, selected one with a monkey holding bananas that read, "Thanks a bunch," and composed a note of gratitude to a teacher who collaborated with me on the aforementioned lesson write-up. Inside the envelope, I placed two organic dark-chocolate squares and wrote, "One treat for you, one treat for someone sweet. Pass it on."

My bottom left-hand drawer has several bags of dark chocolate squares for the purpose of making a chocolate connection. Not a day goes by that I can't genuinely thank a fellow coach, teacher, or administrator. I just need to stop and do it. So I keep a stock of thank-you notes and chocolates to be prepared.

Make It Personal

Some people hate chocolate and I was reminded that not everyone is a fan of "words of affirmation" when I read the book T*he Five Love Languages for Children* by Gary Chapman and Ross Campbell (1997). In simple summary, the book asserts that everyone likes to receive in different ways. At least five ways, in fact: Words of Affirmation, Quality Time, Receiving Gifts, Acts of Service, and Physical Touch. My primary love language is Quality Time; that is, undivided attention meets my needs in a powerful way. I have two secondary love languages. The first is Acts of Service. When my children clean up just so we have a more comfortable space or my husband makes dinner on a Friday because he knows I've had a long week, those acts say, "I care about you" in my language. Then there are Words of Affirmation. An editor of a certain online resource wonderland sends personal handwritten notes that I treasure and that keep me writing.

Love languages in the workplace require some minor revisions. For example, although Physical Touch might be someone's love language, there is less of an opportunity to explore that professionally, leaving us with four:

Words of Affirmation—Written or spoken? There is a difference. Some people love to have their work publicly acknowledged, whereas others (like me) appreciate a thoughtful handwritten note.

Quality Time—Personal or professional? Some educators appreciate the time to talk about their lives outside of school, and others really want to focus on work.

Receiving Gifts—What kind? What do people get energy from? One office professional I worked with loved cinnamon, another treasured fruit juices, still another valued great books. Knowing the difference makes a difference.

Acts of Service—One day many years ago, my principal brought me a cup of steaming hot tea while I was teaching. I've never forgotten that. Good Earth tea, as a matter of fact. Another colleague wrote lesson plans for my substitute so I could rush to be a labor coach for my friend who was giving birth (the day before spring break). That sticks with me, and I think of it when I see her.

Turnaround

Any leadership position in education requires one to communicate with many different people. Some of those people have impeccable communication skills, and even if they disagree with you, they do so respectfully and work toward outcomes that meet both parties' needs. Other educators write emails when they are angry and send them before they think them through. I've received a few of those. One day, two "Januaries" ago, as a matter of fact, I got three of them. I decided that not only was I *not* going to answer those emails until the next day, but I was going to turn the energy around. Three random educators would receive a note of appreciation from me. I closed my eyes to think of what I was grateful for that day. I wrote one note to a teacher I'd passed in the hall who was holding a little girl who had forgotten her lunch. "Thank you," I wrote, "for touching my day with your kindness toward your lunchless student." I wrote another to the PE teacher who had clapped a sixth-grade student on the back and said, "Nice job, man, that's the first time you've ever scored. That's awesome—you are improving." And the third to a new teacher in the district: "I was thinking of you and I'm so glad you were hired. I appreciate your energy and enthusiasm." I left that day with my heart and mind in a hopeful place.

Over time, that's become part of my practice. I take a challenging interaction, a critical email, or even someone rolling their eyes in a meeting, and I turn it around and send it off in a positive way. "When you are grateful, fear disappears and abundance appears" is a quote from Anthony Robbins that describes my experience. Every person in general and teachers in particular benefit from an attitude of gratitude. Thank you, Ahna, for the reminder. I will have an *extcnt* day.

Bibliography

Anderson, Jeff. *Mechanically Inclined: Building Grammar, Usage and Style Into Writer's Workshop.* Portland, ME: Stenhouse, 2005.

———. *Everyday Editing: Inviting Students to Develop Skill and Craft in Writer's Workshop.* Portland, ME: Stenhouse, 2007.

Auch, Mary Jane, and Herm Auch. *The Plot Chickens.* New York: Holiday House, 2009.

Balian, Lorna. *The Aminal.* New York: Star Bright Books, 2005.

Baydo-Reed, Katie. "On Compassion." *Choice Literacy,* September 2011, 1617. http://www.choiceliteracy.com/members/1617.cfm.

Beals, Kevin. *My Nature Notebook.* Seeds of Science, Roots of Reading Series. Nashua, NH: Delta Education, 2008.

Beers, Kylene. *Why Kids Can't Read: What Teacher Can Do: A Guide for Teachers 6–12.* Portsmouth, NH: Heinemann, 2003.

Bishop, Nic. *Frogs.* New York: Scholastic, 2008.

Boushey, Gail, and Joan Moser. *The Daily Five: Fostering Literacy Independence in the Elementary Grades.* Portland, ME: Stenhouse, 2006.

Burns, Marilyn. *Writing in Math Class: A Resource for Grades 2–8.* Sausalito, CA: Math Solutions Publications, 1995.

Cambourne, Brian. "Toward an Educationally Relevant Theory of Literacy Learning: Twenty Years of Inquiry." *The Reading Teacher* 49, no. 3 (1995): 182–190.

Casey, Katherine. *Literacy Coaching: The Essentials.* Portsmouth, NH: Heinemann, 2006.

Chamberlin, Mary, and Rich Chamberlin. *Mama Panya's Pancakes.* Cambridge, MA: Barefoot Books, 2005.

Chapman, Gary, and Ross Campbell, M.D. *The Five Love Languages of Children.* Chicago: Northfield, 1997.

Cisneros, Sandra. *The House on Mango Street.* New York: Vintage, 1989.

Clements, Andrew. *Frindle.* New York: Simon and Schuster, 1996.

Curwin, Richard L., Allen N. Mendler, and Brian D. Mendler. *Discipline with Dignity: New Challenges, New Solutions.* Alexandria, VA: Association for Supervision and Curriculum Development, 2008.

DuFour, Rebecca, Richard DuFour, Robert Eaker, and Thomas Many. *Learning by Doing: A Handbook for Professional Learning Communities at Work.* Bloomington, IN: Solution Tree Press, 2006.

Finchler, Judy. *Testing Miss Malarkey.* New York: Walker, 2000.

Fleischman, Paul. *Joyful Noise: Poems for Two Voices.* New York: A Charlotte Zolotow Book, 1988.

Fletcher, Ralph, and JoAnn Portalupi. *Writing Workshop: The Essential Guide.* Portsmouth, NH: Heinemann, 2001.

Fogarty, Mignon. "Grammar Girl: Appositives: Quick and Dirty Tips." *Grammar Girl.* Last modified October 17, 2008. http://grammar .quickanddirtytips.com/appositives.aspx.

Ginott, Dr. Haim G., Dr. Alice Ginott, and Dr. H. Wallace Goddard. *Between Parent and Child.* New York: Three Rivers Press, 2003.

Hattie, John A. C. *Visible Learning: A Synthesis of Meta-analyses Relating to Achievement.* New York: Routledge, 2009.

Johnston, Peter H. *Choice Words.* Portland, ME: Stenhouse, 2004.

King, Bruce M., and John H. Gunn. "Trouble in Paradise: Power, Conflict and Community in an Interdisciplinary Teaching Team." http://uex.sagepub.com/content/38/2/173.abstract

Kissner, Emily. *Summarizing, Paraphrasing, and Retelling: Skills for Better Reading, Writing, and Test Taking.* Portsmouth, NH: Heinemann, 2006.

Lipton, Laura, EdD, and Bruce Wellman, MEd. *Mentoring Matters: A Practical Guide to Learning-Focused Relationships.* N.p.: MiraVia LLC, 2003.

Litwin, Eric. *Pete the Cat.* New York: Harper Collins, 2008.

Marzano, Robert J., Debra J. Pickering and Jane E. Pollock. *Classroom Instruction That Works: Research-Based Strategies for Increasing Student Achievement.* Alexandria, VA: Association for Supervision and Curriculum Development, 2001.

Marzano, Robert J., Debra J. Pickering, and Jana S. Marzano. *Classroom Management That Works: Research-Based Strategies for Every Teacher.* Alexandria, VA: Association for Supervision and Curriculum Development, 2003.

Marzano, Robert J., Jennifer S. Norford, Diane E. Paynter, Debra J. Pickering, and Barbara B. Gaddy. *A Handbook of Classroom Instruction That Works.* Alexandria, VA: Association for Supervision and Curriculum Development, 2004.

McCully, Emily Arnold. *Marvelous Mattie: How Margaret E. Knight Became an Inventor.* Toronto, Canada: Douglas & McIntyre, 2006.

Prap, Lila. *Why?* La Jolla, CA: Kane Miller, 2005.

Ray, Katie Wood, and Matt Glover. *Already Ready: Nurturing Writers in Preschool and Kindergarten.* Portsmouth, NH: Heinemann, 2008.

Rosenberg, Marshall B., PhD. *Nonviolent Communication: A Language of Life.* Encinitas, CA: Puddle Dancer Press, 2003.

Rowe, Mary Budd. "Wait Time: Slowing Down May Be a Way of Speeding Up!" *Journal of Teacher Education* 37, no. 43 (January 1986): 43–50.

Siddons, Suzy. *The Complete Presentation Skills Handbook.* Kogan Page, 2008.

Spandel, Vicki. *Creating Writers Through 6-Trait Writing Assessment and Instruction.* Boston: Pearson, 2005.

Sweeney, Diane. *Student-Centered Coaching: A Guide for K–8 Coaches and Principals.* Thousand Oaks, CA: Corwin, 2011.

"Washington Laws." The Safety Restraint Coalition. Last modified January–February 2012. http://www.800bucklup.org/laws/index.asp.

Willems, Mo. *Elephants Cannot Dance.* New York: Hyperion, 2009.

Wong, Harry K., and Rosemary T. Wong. *The First Days of School: How to Be an Effective Teacher.* Mountain View, CA: Harry K. Wong Productions, 2009.

Zinsser, William. *Writing to Learn.* New York: Harper and Row, 1988.